TYPE 2 DIABETES COOKBOOK FOR BEGINNERS

1000 days of Delicious and Mouthwatering Recipes for Newly Diagnosed With 1-Month Meal Plan to Lower Your Sugar and Empower Your Wellness.

© **Copyright 2022 - All rights reserved.**

The content contained within this book may not be reproduced, duplicated or transmitted without direct written permission from the author or the publisher.
Under no circumstances will any blame or legal responsibility be held against the publisher, or author, for any damages, reparation, or monetary loss due to the information contained within this book. Either directly or indirectly.

Legal Notice:
This book is copyright protected. This book is only for personal use. You cannot amend, distribute, sell, use, quote or paraphrase any part, or the content within this book, without the consent of the author or publisher.

Disclaimer Notice:
Please note the information contained within this document is for educational and entertainment purposes only. All effort has been executed to present accurate, up to date, and reliable, complete information. No warranties of any kind are declared or implied. Readers acknowledge that the author is not engaging in the rendering of legal, financial, medical or professional advice. The content within this book has been derived from various sources. Please consult a licensed professional before attempting any techniques outlined in this book.
By reading this document, the reader agrees that under no circumstances is the author responsible for any losses, direct or indirect, which are incurred because of the use of information contained within this document, including, but not limited to, errors, omissions, or inaccuracies.

Table of Contents

INTRODUCTION 5
DIFFERENCE BETWEEN TYPE 1 AND 2 DIABETES 6
30-DAY MEAL PLAN 8
BREAKFAST 10
1. Bell Peppered Rings with Egg and Avocado Salsa 10
2. Apple Cinnamon Chia Pudding 10
3. Veggie Fillets Omelets 11
4. Raspberry Choco Oatmeal 11
5. Salad with Salsa Verde Vinaigrette 12
6. Cottage Pancakes 12
7. Greek Yogurt and Oat Pancakes 12
8. Apple and Pumpkin Waffles 13
9. Buckwheat Crêpes 13
10. Mushroom Frittata 14
11. Tropical Yogurt Kiwi Bowl 14
12. Banana Crêpe Cakes 14
13. Tacos with Pico De Gallo 15
14. Portobello and Chicken Sausage Frittata 15
15. Egg Salad Sandwiches 16
16. Shrimp with Scallion Grits 16
17. Breakfast Cheddar Zucchini Casserole 16
18. Banana and Zucchini Bread 17
19. Breakfast Grain Porridge 17
20. Tomato Waffles 17

LUNCH 19
21. Green Salad with Berries and Sweet Potatoes 19
22. Three Bean and Scallion Salad 20
23. Rainbow Bean Salad 20
24. Warm Barley and Squash Salad 20
25. Citrus and Chicken Salad 21
26. Blueberry and Chicken Salad 21
27. Joseph's Bacon 22
28. Texas Goulash 22
29. Roasted Chickpea 22
30. Coconut Meringue Cake 23
31. Banana Nut Bread 23
32. Oyster Stew 23
33. Pecan-Oatmeal Pancakes 24
34. Basic Bread Stuffing 24
35. Dill Pickle Dip 24
36. Funnel Cakes 25
37. Shrimp Burgers 25
38. Whole Wheat Chapatti 25
39. Sugar Free Strawberry Cheesecake 26
40. Shrimps Saganaki 26

DINNER 26
41. Cilantro and Lime Broccoli Rice 27
42. Spicy Garlic Pasta 28
43. Simple Beef Roast 28
44. Honey Garlic Butter Roasted Carrots 28
45. Colorful vegetable casserole 28
46. Lentil snack with Tomato salsa 29
47. Clear soup with liver dumplings 29
48. Beef steaks with green asparagus 30
49. Broccoli Omelet 30
50. Apple Cinnamon Oatmeal 31
51. Nutty Steel-cut Oatmeal with Blueberries 31
52. Slow "Roasted" Tomatoes 31
53. Tomato-Herb Omelet 32
54. Mouth-Watering Egg Casserole 32
55. Amazing Overnight Apple and Cinnamon Oatmeal 33
56. Zoodles with Pea Pesto 33
57. Shrimp Peri-Peri 33
58. Halibut with Lime and Cilantro 34
59. Autumn Pork Chop with Red Cabbage and Apples 34
60. Orange-Marinated Pork Tenderloin 34

MEAT 36
61. Pork Medallions with Cherry Sauce 36
62. Pork Chops Pomodoro 36
63. Meatballs Barley Soup 37
64. Beef Massaman Curry 37
65. Old Fashioned Beef Soup with Vegetables 38
66. Beef and Red Bean Chili 38
67. Cider Pork Stew 39
68. Cuban Pulled Pork Sandwich 39
69. Sunday Pot Roast 40
70. Broccoli Beef Stir-Fry 40
71. Beef and Pepper Fajita Bowls 41
72. Meat skewers with polenta 41
73. Chipotle Chili Pork Chops 42
74. Lime-Parsley Lamb Cutlets 42
75. Traditional Beef Stroganoff 42
76. Smothered Sirloin 43
77. Loaded Cottage Pie 43
78. Fresh Pot Pork Butt 44
79. Pork Diane 44
80. Autumn Pork Chops 45

POULTRY 46
81. Turkey Chili 46
82. Barbecue Turkey Burger Sliders 47
83. Turkey and Quinoa Caprese Casserole 47
84. Turkey Divan Casserole 48
85. Spiced Chicken Breast 48
86. Seasoned Chicken Breast 48
87. Bruschetta Chicken 49
88. Chicken with Caper Sauce 49
89. Yogurt and Parmesan Chicken Bake 49
90. Pesto Chicken Bake 50
91. Chicken and Broccoli Bake 50
92. Chicken and Veggies Bake 50
93. Chicken with Olives 51
94. Chicken with Bell Peppers 51
95. Chicken with Bok Choy 52
96. Chicken with Cabbage 52
97. Chicken with Mushrooms 52
98. Chicken with Broccoli and Mushroom 53
99. Chicken with Zucchini Noodles 53
100. Chicken with Yellow Squash 53

FISH AND SEAFOOD 55
101. Salmon Cakes 55
102. Coconut Shrimp 55
103. Crispy Fish Sticks 56
104. Honey-Glazed Salmon 56
105. Basil-Parmesan Crusted Salmon 57
106. Cajun Shrimp 57
107. Crispy Air Fryer Fish 57

#	Recipe	Page
108.	Air Fryer Lemon Cod	58
109.	Salmon Fillets	58
110.	Fish and Chips	58
111.	Grilled Salmon with Lemon	58
112.	Fish Nuggets	59
113.	Garlic Rosemary Grilled Prawns	59
114.	Cajun Catfish	59
115.	Cajun Flounder and Tomatoes	60
116.	Cajun Shrimp and Roasted Vegetables	60
117.	Cilantro Lime Grilled Shrimp	60
118.	Crab Frittata	62
119.	Crunchy Lemon Shrimp	62
120.	Grilled Tuna Steaks	62

VEGGIES **63**

#	Recipe	Page
121.	Baked Zucchini Recipe from Mexico	63
122.	Banana Pepper Stuffed with Tofu 'n Spices	64
123.	Baked Potato Topped with Cream cheese 'n Olives	64
124.	Brussels sprouts with Balsamic Oil	64
125.	Bell Pepper-Corn Wrapped in Tortilla	65
126.	Black Bean Burger with Garlic-Chipotle	65
127.	Vegan Edamame Quinoa Collard Wraps	65
128.	Baked Eggplant with Marinara	66
129.	Crispy-Topped Baked Vegetables	66
130.	Creamy Spinach and Mushroom Lasagna	67
131.	Zucchini Parmesan Chips	67
132.	Roasted Squash Puree	68
133.	Roasted Root Vegetables	68
134.	Hummus	68
135.	Thai Roasted Veggies	69
136.	Cheesy Cauliflower Fritters	69
137.	Crispy Jalapeno Coins	69
138.	Jicama Fries	70
139.	Air Fryer Brussels sprouts	70
140.	Spaghetti Squash Tots	70

SNACKS **71**

#	Recipe	Page
141.	Chicken and Mushrooms	71
142.	Cheeseburger Pie	72
143.	Salmon Feta and Pesto Wrap	72
144.	Salmon Cream Cheese and Onion on Bagel	72
145.	Melon Cucumber Salad	73
146.	Greek Baklava	73
147.	Glazed Bananas in Phyllo Nut Cups	73
148.	Salmon Apple Salad Sandwich	74
149.	Smoked Salmon and Cheese on Rye Bread	74
150.	Pan-Fried Trout	74
151.	Lemon Cream Fruit Dip	75
152.	Greek Salad Kabobs	75
153.	Green Goddess White Bean Dip	75
154.	Vietnamese Meatball Lollipops with Dipping Sauce	76
155.	Blackberry Baked Brie	76
156.	Creamy Spinach Dip	77
157.	Pesto Veggie Pizza	77
158.	Apple Leather	78
159.	French bread Pizza	78
160.	Candied Pecans	78

SIDE DISHES **80**

#	Recipe	Page
161.	French Lentils	80
162.	Grain-Free Berry Cobbler	81
163.	Coffee-Steamed Carrots	81
164.	Rosemary Potatoes	81
165.	Kale and Cabbage Salad with Peanuts	82
166.	Chili Lime Salmon	82
167.	Collard Greens	82
168.	Mashed Pumpkin	83
169.	Turkey Loaf	83
170.	Mushroom Pasta	83
171.	Garlic Kale Chips	84
172.	Garlic Salmon Balls	84
173.	Onion Rings	84
174.	Crispy Eggplant Fries	85
175.	Charred Bell Peppers	85
176.	Garlic Tomatoes	85
177.	Mushroom Stew	85
178.	Cheese and Onion Nuggets	86
179.	Spiced Nuts	86
180.	Keto French fries	86

APPETIZER **87**

#	Recipe	Page
181.	Calico Slaw	87
182.	Simple Appetizer Meatballs	87
183.	Chicken Souvlaki Salad	88
184.	Celery with Chickpea Feta Salad	88
185.	Basil Vinaigrette with Summer Corn Salad	88
186.	Lemon Vinaigrette with Sugar Snap Pea Salad	89
187.	Green Dressing with Shrimp Avocado Salad	89
188.	Beans with Pearl Couscous	90
189.	Blackened Chicken Breast with Jalapeno Caesar Salad	91
190.	Ginger Dressing with Kale Chicken Salad	91
191.	Asian Cucumber Salad	91
192.	Pecans with Blackberry Ginger Beet Salad	91
193.	Blueberry Watermelon Salad	92
194.	Orange Vinaigrette with Roasted Beets	92
195.	Blueberries with Nectarines Spinach Salad	93
196.	Taco Slaw	93
197.	Egg Fried Veg	93
198.	Bone Broth	93
199.	Cauliflower and Celeriac Soup	94
200.	Mushroom and Eggs	94

DESSERT **95**

#	Recipe	Page
201.	Strawberry Chiffon Pie	95
202.	Strawberry Fruit Squares	95
203.	Copper Penny Carrots	95
204.	Poached Pears	96
205.	Carrot Cake	96
206.	Bran Muffins	96
207.	Frozen Mocha Milkshake	97
208.	Baked Berry Cups with Crispy Cinnamon Wedges	97
209.	Berry Smoothie Pops	98
210.	Instant Pot Tapioca	98
211.	Oatmeal Cookies	100
212.	Raspberry Nice Cream	100
213.	Chocolate Baked Bananas	100
214.	Greek Yogurt Berry Smoothie Pops	100
215.	Grilled Peach and Coconut Yogurt Bowls	100
216.	Frozen Chocolate Peanut Butter Bites	100
217.	Dark Chocolate Almond Butter Cups	100
218.	No-Bake Carrot Cake Bites	100
219.	Creamy Strawberry Crepes	100
220.	Swirled Cream Cheese Brownies	100

INDEX **10**

CONCLUSION **10**

Introduction

Diabetes is a disease caused by either insufficient hormone insulin or the body's inability to react to insulin. Some of the known symptoms of diabetes are excessive thirst, weight loss or gain, blurred vision, frequent urination, and slow healing wounds. Type 2 diabetes accounts for approximately 95% of all cases of diabetes. Type 2 Diabetes usually develops in adults and can last for a lifetime. It was once thought that diabetes only affected older people. However, this is not true. Both type 1 and 2 diabetes can begin at any age. The risk of developing diabetes increases as the person ages, so the condition is more common in adults. Type 2 Diabetes develops from a lack of insulin from the pancreas or insulin resistance of the body's cells. A combination of facts may play a role in causing this disease, including genetics, lifestyle habits, infections, and age. Diabetes is also linked with obesity. Type 2 Diabetes is led by an imbalance between the amount of insulin produced by the pancreas and the body's cells. The cell's insulin receptors are not working as efficiently as they should, so the body cannot utilize the insulin being formed by the pancreas. Too much sugar promotes up in the blood, which leads to other complications.

Prevention of the development of type 2 diabetes is possible if one adheres to a healthy lifestyle. Losing excess weight can help to prevent type 2 diabetes. Exercise, a healthy diet, and proper sleep each day contribute to good health. Controlling risk factors that lead to type 2 diabetes can also help keep this disease at bay. Risk factors include:

High cholesterol levels.
High blood pressure.
High blood sugar levels.
Being overweight or obese.

Life for someone with diabetes is not easy. With the help of this book, your body will learn to use stored fat as energy and eventually begin using the sugar circulating in your blood. Once you manage your blood sugar levels naturally, you'll be able to reduce or even eliminate your diabetes medications. You can retrieve control of your metabolism and reach optimal health. Healthy foods will be easy to include in your diet. Your body will begin to role at its optimal weight and become more energy efficient. You will feel more energetic and become more aware of what your body needs. This book aims to make your life easier by showing you how simple it can be. If you are existing with or caring for someone with diabetes, this book has information that will help you stay healthy and happy along the way. This cookbook will show you how to use healthy ingredients to create delicious, satisfying meals for the entire family.

After reading this book, you will apprehend how Type 2 diabetes develops and make better choices for yourself. The recipes in this cookbook will assist you prepare creative, great-tasting meals that are healthy and easy on your budget. What are you waiting for? Now is the time to make a transform, and these recipes are your guide to helping your diabetes improve.

Difference between Type 1 and 2 Diabetes

When you first hear the term "Type 2 Diabetes", it may seem like some new disease only recently discovered. Still, Type 1 and Type 2 diabetes are two different diseases with different symptoms and complications.

Diabetes is usually either type 1 or type 2, although these two subtypes can also be concurrent within an individual.

Type 1 diabetes (known as insulin-dependent diabetes) has nothing to do with insulin. Still, it is an autoimmune disease where the immune system destroys the beta cells in the pancreas. Type 1 is usually diagnosed before 20 years of age, and it requires daily injections of insulin to stay alive. Unlike Type 2, this is led by genetics and lifestyle factors, Type 1 results from a genetic defect in the pancreas. This means that there will be no danger of complications even if patients discontinue their insulin.

Type 2 diabetes (previously called non-insulin-dependent or adult-onset diabetes) happens more commonly in adults over 40 years. This may be taught that adult-onset diabetes is associated with weight gain and a sedentary lifestyle.

How to Prevent Diabetes and Control Sugar Level

Preventing diabetes sounds like an obvious statement to make, but it is also one of the most important ways to reduce your risk. Lowering your body weight and maintaining a healthy diet will help you prevent diabetes. One of the most common causes of high blood sugar levels is eating too many carbohydrates. So, reducing the intake of carbohydrates will help you reduce your blood sugar level within a few days.

As long as you manage a healthy lifestyle, there are no reasons to take medications or supplements that may cause further complications in the future.

Additional Information Regarding Nutritional Goals for Type 2 Diabetic Patients

People with type 2 diabetes are also encouraged to maintain physical activity to reduce the risk of long-term complications of this disease. Another way to gain effective control of blood sugar levels is by restricting your calorie intake. This means that you should maximize the number of foods that are rich in carbohydrates. Fruits and vegetables are essential parts of a healthy diet. So, if you want to lower the risk of several diseases, including type 2 diabetes, you should insert these foods into your daily meals. By following a healthy diet and maintaining a healthy lifestyle, people with type 2 diabetes can slow down the development of complications and prevent long-term side effects.

The Relationship between Nutrients and Diabetes

By eating healthy foods, you can reduce your risk of complications caused by diabetes. Nutrients have a significant impact on blood sugar levels, which is the leading cause of complications of this disease. While it is recommended to eat healthy foods, some individuals rely solely on medications or supplements to manage their blood sugar levels. Dietary therapy aims to establish a nutrition plan that lowers blood sugar levels and maintains healthy cells. To support this goal, you can use several sources of carbohydrate while still managing your sugar level.

What to Avoid and What to Eat

Forbidden foods are not recommended for people who have diabetes. The most common foods considered forbidden are sugar (including beverages), alcohol, and trans-fat, while carbohydrates should be limited to 250-275 grams per day. Some other food items that are high in calories and can be dangerous for the diabetic individual are meats and cheese. The list of these foods is long, but there are a few unusual examples that we will look at:

- Sweetened beverages: They contain sugar, sometimes a lot of sugar. So, they a must no. Replace with just water or unsweetened tea.
- Bacon: Bacon is another meat item not recommended for people with diabetes. Bacon contains a lot of saturated fat, which can be dangerous for people with diabetes. In general fish and white meat (not canned!) are more friendly to people suffering from diabetes.
- Processed Cheese (or processed cheese products): Processed cheese companies use artificial ingredients to manufacture their products and thus are not advised for people with diabetes. Unfortunately, there is no substitute for processed cheese so this is something that most diabetics must avoid at all costs. Better low fat and fresh cheese.
- Red Meat: Red meats are considered forbidden foods for people with diabetes. Red meat contains a lot of cholesterol which on digestion turns into lousy cholesterol in the body. Harmful cholesterol levels may lead to the formation of blood clots in the body.
- White Rice: White rice is packed with carbohydrates, and not much fiber or other nutrition value is found in white rice. These properties make white rice a forbidden food for people with diabetes.

- Fried Potato: The fried potato is not suitable for people with diabetes because fried potatoes contain many calories and carbohydrates. Fried potato is not as bad as white rice, but it should be avoided like any other food item in the diet of a diabetic person.

Superfoods for Diabetic- Superfoods are any food item that contains high nutrition and low carbohydrate content. These foods are healthy and nutritious and must be included in the diabetic diet plan.

These are the foods that can be included in the diet of a diabetic person.

- Fish- Fish is a high protein and low carbohydrate food. Fish contains omega-3 fatty acids, which are suitable for the cardiovascular system.
- Salmon- This is a perfect fish recommended for people with diabetes because salmon contains omega-3 fatty acids, which are suitable for the blood sugar level of a person with diabetes.
- Nuts and Nut butter- Nuts are one of the best and most healthy food items. Many people with diabetes prefer to have nuts because they contain a lot of fat which is a suitable type of fat that helps lower cholesterol levels in the body.
- Avocados- Avocados are rich in fiber which can be very good for health due to their high fiber content.
- Green Tea- Green tea contains antioxidants which can be very good for the health of diabetic people.
- Oatmeal- Oatmeal is one of the best food items for people with diabetes. Oatmeal is low in calories, contains a lot of fiber, and is a good source of vitamins and minerals.
- Whole grains are another excellent food item that has become very popular these days because they taste so good and are very nutritious as well. Whole grains contain more fiber which helps in keeping blood sugar levels under control.
- Mushrooms- Mushrooms contain minimal amount of carbohydrates and are very high in nutrition value.
- Yogurt- White and low-fat yogurt is also a good food item for people with diabetes. It contains probiotics, which are suitable for gut health in general. Probiotics are good bacteria that help maintain a healthy digestive system.
- Olive Oil- Olive oil contains monounsaturated fats, considered the best type of fat for a person who has diabetes. Monounsaturated fats help in reducing the cholesterol level in the blood of a diabetic person.
- Broccoli- Broccoli is included in the list of superfoods because it contains rich amounts of vitamins and minerals and is very low in carbohydrates.

Discouraged or limited food- Many foods may have limited or unwanted effects on the body, but this does not mean that they are entirely inappropriate for people with diabetes. When eating foods that are considered discouraged, it is essential that the nutritionist knows about all possible interactions caused by diabetics in advance.

The following foods are discouraged or limited from the menu of a diabetic person:

- Fruits- Diabetic person should take at least 2 servings of fruit daily. It is recommended that fruits that are rich in fiber and low in sugar be eaten during the day. Better to avoid dried, canned, sirup fruits.
- Fats- It is advised that a diabetic person must limit his consumption of fats to less than 30% of his calorie intake per day. Also, foods that contain trans-fat should be avoided at all costs.
- Carbohydrates. They should be limited to 250-275 gr per day and better if coming from not processed flours.
- Sweeteners- It is advised that diabetic individuals use sweeteners like Splenda and Stevia instead of the traditional table sugar.

30-Day Meal Plan

DAY	BREAKFAST	LUNCH	DINNER	SNACK
Day-1	Bell Peppered Rings with Egg and Avocado Salsa	Green Salad with Berries and Sweet Potatoes	Cilantro and Lime Broccoli Rice	Chicken and Mushrooms
Day-2	Apple Cinnamon Chia Pudding	Three Bean and Scallion Salad	Spicy Garlic Pasta	Cheeseburger Pie
Day-3	Veggie Fillets Omelets	Rainbow Bean Salad	Simple Beef Roast	Salmon Feta and Pesto Wrap
Day-4	Raspberry Choco Oatmeal	Warm Barley and Squash Salad	Honey Garlic Butter Roasted Carrots	Salmon Cream Cheese and Onion on Bagel
Day-5	Salad with Salsa Verde Vinaigrette	Citrus and Chicken Salad	Colorful vegetable casserole	Melon Cucumber Salad
Day-6	Cottage Pancakes	Blueberry and Chicken Salad	Lentil snack with tomato salsa	Greek Baklava
Day-7	Greek Yogurt and Oat Pancakes	Joseph's Bacon	Clear soup with liver dumplings	Glazed Bananas in Phyllo Nut Cups
Day-8	Apple and Pumpkin Waffles	Texas Goulash	Beef steaks with green asparagus	Salmon Apple Salad Sandwich
Day-9	Buckwheat Crêpes	Roasted Chickpea	Broccoli Omelet	Smoked Salmon and Cheese on Rye Bread
Day-10	Mushroom Frittata	Coconut Meringue Cake	Apple Cinnamon Oatmeal	Pan-Fried Trout
Day-11	Tropical Yogurt Kiwi Bowl	Banana Nut Bread	Nutty Steel-cut Oatmeal with Blueberries	Lemon Cream Fruit Dip
Day-12	Banana Crêpe Cakes	Oyster Stew	Slow "Roasted" Tomatoes	Greek Salad Kabobs
Day-13	Tacos with Pico De Gallo	Pecan-Oatmeal Pancakes	Tomato-Herb Omelet	Green Goddess White Bean Dip
Day-14	Portobello and Chicken Sausage Frittata	Basic Bread Stuffing	Mouth-Watering Egg Casserole	Vietnamese Meatball Lollipops with Dipping Sauce
Day-15	Egg Salad Sandwiches	Dill Pickle Dip	Amazing Overnight Apple and Cinnamon Oatmeal	Blackberry Baked Brie
Day-16	Shrimp with Scallion Grits	Funnel Cakes	Zoodles with Pea Pesto	Creamy Spinach Dip
Day-17	Breakfast Cheddar Zucchini Casserole	Shrimp Burgers	Shrimp Peri-Peri	Pesto Veggie Pizza
Day-18	Banana and Zucchini Bread	Whole Wheat Chapatti	Halibut with Lime and Cilantro	Apple Leather
Day-19	Breakfast Grain Porridge	Sugar Free Strawberry Cheesecake	Autumn Pork Chop with Red Cabbage and Apples	French bread Pizza
Day-20	Tomato Waffles	Shrimps Saganaki	Orange-Marinated Pork Tenderloin	Candied Pecans

Day-21	Greek Yogurt and Oat Pancakes	Pork Chops Pomodoro	Baked Zucchini Recipe from Mexico	Hummus
Day-22	Portobello and Chicken Sausage Frittata	Beef and Pepper Fajita Bowls	Thai Roasted Veggies	Frozen Mocha Milkshake
Day-23	Banana and Zucchini Bread	Salmon Fillets	Spaghetti Squash Tots	Bruschetta Chicken
Day-24	Apple and Pumpkin Waffles	Beef and Red Bean Chili	Roasted Squash Puree	Jicama Fries
Day-25	Raspberry Choco Oatmeal	Fish Nuggets	Garlic Rosemary Grilled Prawns	Vegan Edamame Quinoa Collard Wraps
Day-26	Mushroom Frittata	Pest Chicken Bake	Chicken with Cabbage	Garlic Kale Chips
Day-27	Cottage Pancakes	Crab Frittata	Baked Eggplants with Marinara	Crispy Jalapen Coins
Day-28	Tropical Yogurt Kiwi Bowl	Turkey Chili	Crispy Fish Sticks	Onion Rings
Day-29	Shrimp with Scallion Grits	Cider Pork Stew	Chicken with Mushrooms	Zucchini Parmesan Chips
Day-30	Breakfast Grain Porridge	Chicken with Olives	Brussels Sprouts with Balsamic Oil	Oatmeal Cookies

Breakfast

1. Bell Peppered Rings with Egg and Avocado Salsa

Preparation Time: 20 minutes   **Cooking Time:** 40 minutes   **Servings:** 12

Ingredients:
- 2 tomatoes, seeded and diced
- Juice of 1 lime
- ¾ teaspoon of salt, divided
- 2 teaspoons of olive oil, divided
- 8 large eggs
- 2 bell peppers of any color
- 1 avocado, diced
- ½ cup of diced red onion
- 1 jalapeño pepper, minced
- ½ cup plus more for garnish of chopped fresh cilantro
- ¼ teaspoon of ground pepper, divided

Directions:
1. Slice the bottoms and tops off bell peppers, and then finely dice.
2. Remove and discard membranes and seeds.
3. Slice each pepper into four half-inch thick rings.
4. Combine the diced pepper with onion, avocado, cilantro, jalapeno, lime juice, tomatoes, and half a teaspoon of salt in a medium bowl.
5. In a large nonstick skillet, warmth about 1 teaspoon of oil over medium heat.
6. Add 4 bell pepper rings, and then crack about 1 egg into the middle of each ring.
7. Season with ⅛ teaspoon of each pepper and salt.
8. Cook and flip gentle. Transfer into serving plates.
9. Repeat with the rest of the pepper rings and eggs.
10. Serve and enjoy!

Nutrition:
Calories: 285   Carbohydrates: 14.2g   Sugar: 5.9g
Protein: 15.1g   Dietary Fiber: 5.9g   Fat: 19.5g

2. Apple Cinnamon Chia Pudding

Preparation Time: 10 minutes   **Cooking Time:** 8 hours (refrigerate)   **Servings:** 1

Ingredients:
- ¼ teaspoon of vanilla extract
- ¼ teaspoon of ground cinnamon
- ½ cup of diced apple, divided
- ½ cup of unsweetened milk or other nondairy milk
- 2 tablespoons of chia seeds
- 2 teaspoons of pure maple syrup

- 1 tablespoon of chopped toasted pecans, divided

Directions:
1. In a small bowl, stir chia, almond milk (or other non-dairy milk), maple syrup, chia, cinnamon, and vanilla.
2. Cover and refrigerate for about 8 hours and up to 3 days.
3. Stir well when ready to serve.
4. Spoon about half of the pudding into a serving bowl or glass.
5. Top with half the pecans and apple.
6. Add the rest of the pudding.
7. Top with the rest of the pecans and apples.
8. Serve and enjoy!

Nutrition:
Calories: 233
Protein: 4.8g
Carbohydrates: 27.7g
Dietary Fiber: 10.1g
Sugar: 14.4g
Fat: 12.7g

3. Veggie Fillets Omelets

Preparation Time: 5 minutes **Cooking Time:** 30 minutes **Servings:** 4

Ingredients:
- ½ ripe avocado, pitted, peeled, and chopped
- 2 eggs
- 1 cup of refrigerated or frozen egg product,
- 2 tablespoons of water
- 1 snipped fresh chive
- 1 teaspoon of dried basil, crushed
- ¼ teaspoon of salt
- ½ cup of no-salt-added diced tomatoes with garlic, basil, and oregano, well-drained
- ½ cup of cucumber, chopped and seeded
- ½ cup of yellow summer squash
- ¼ teaspoon of ground black pepper
- Nonstick cooking spray
- ¼ cup of shredded reduced-fat Monterey Jack cheese with jalapeño chili peppers

Directions:
For the filling:
1. Mix the tomatoes, cucumber, squash, and avocado in a bowl and set aside.

For each of the omelets:
1. Use the cooking spray in a non-stick skillet.
2. Heat it over medium heat and add about ⅓ cup of the egg mixture.
3. Stir the eggs immediately and continuously until the mixture resembles cooked egg pieces surrounded by liquid eggs.
4. Cook until done for about 30 to 60 seconds.
2. Whisk together the eggs, salt, water, basil, and pepper in a medium bowl.
5. Spoon about ½ cup of the filling onto one side of the omelet.
6. Fold the omelet over the filling and remove the omelet from the pan.
7. Repeat to make about 4 omelets total, wiping the pan between each omelet.
8. Sprinkle about a tbsp. of cheese over each omelet (to taste). Garnish with chives, then serve and enjoy!

Nutrition:
Calories: 128
Protein: 12.3g
Carbohydrates: 6.7g
Dietary Fiber: 3.5g
Sugars: 4.1g
Fat 6.1g

4. Raspberry Choco Oatmeal

Preparation Time: 10 minutes **Cooking Time:** 20 minutes **Servings:** 4

Ingredients:
- 3 cups of unsweetened almond milk
- 1 cup of fresh red raspberries
- 1-½ cups of regular rolled oats
- 2 tablespoons of unsweetened cocoa powder
- ¼ teaspoon of salt
- 4 teaspoons of sugar-free chocolate-flavor syrup (Optional)

Directions:
1. Mix the salt, oats, and cocoa powder in a saucepan.
2. Add the almonds and milk.
3. Set to a boil over medium heat, stirring occasionally.
4. Lower the heat and simmer until thick, about 5 to 7 minutes, stirring.
5. Cover and remove from heat.
6. Allow resting for about 3 minutes.
7. Divide the oatmeal mixture among 4 bowls.
8. Set each serving with about ¼ cup raspberries.
9. On top of each serving, sprinkle with 1 teaspoon of chocolate syrup (to taste). Serve and enjoy!

Nutrition:

Calories: 157	Carbohydrates: 26.2g	Sugars: 2.2g
Protein: 5.4g	Dietary Fiber: 6.6g	Fat: 4.7g

5. Salad with Salsa Verde Vinaigrette

Preparation Time: 10 minutes **Cooking Time:** 0 minutes **Servings:** 1

Ingredients:
- 2 cups of mesclun / other salad greens
- 8 blue corn tortilla chips, set into large pieces
- ½ cup of canned red kidney beans, rinsed
- ¼ avocado, sliced
- 3 tablespoons of salsa verde, such as Frontera brand
- 1 tablespoon plus 1 teaspoon of extra-virgin olive oil divided
- 2 tablespoons of chopped cilantro, plus more for garnish
- 1 large egg

Directions:
1. Blend the sauce, cilantro and use foil in a small bowl.
2. Mix about half of the mixture with the mesclun in a bowl.
3. Layer the chips, beans, and avocado on top of the salad.
4. Over medium-high heat, heat 1 teaspoon oil in a small nonstick skillet.
5. Add the egg and fry for about ⅔ minutes until the white is cooked, but the yolk is still slightly runny.
6. Serve the egg on top of the salad.
7. Drizzle with the rest of the vinaigrette.
8. Sprinkle with the rest of the cilantro (to taste). Serve and enjoy!

Nutrition:

Calories: 526	Carbohydrates: 36g	Sugars: 3g
Protein: 17g	Dietary Fiber: 14g	Fat: 33g

6. Cottage Pancakes

Preparation Time: 10 minutes **Cooking Time:** 20 minutes **Servings:** 4

Ingredients:
- 2 cups low-fat cottage cheese
- 4 egg whites
- 2 eggs
- 1 tablespoon pure vanilla extract
- 1½ cups almond flour
- Nonstick cooking spray

Directions:
1. Set the cottage cheese, egg whites, eggs, and vanilla in a blender and pulse to combine.
2. Attach the almond flour to the blender and blend until smooth.
3. Set a large nonstick skillet and lightly coat it with cooking spray.
4. Set ¼ cup of batter per pancake, 4 at a time, into the skillet. Cook the pancakes until the bottoms are firm and golden, about 4 minutes.
5. Flip and cook the other side until they are cooked through, about 3 minutes.
6. Detach the pancakes to a plate and repeat with the remaining batter.
7. Serve with fresh fruit.

Nutrition:

Calories: 345	Carbohydrates: 11.1g	Sodium: 560mg
Fat: 22.1g	Fiber: 4.1g	
Protein: 29.1g	Sugar: 5.1g	

7. Greek Yogurt and Oat Pancakes

Preparation Time: 5 minutes **Cooking Time:** 20 minutes **Servings:** 4

Ingredients:
- 1 cup 2 percent plain Greek yogurt
- 3 eggs
- 1½ teaspoons pure vanilla extract
- 1 cup rolled oats
- 1 tablespoon granulated sweetener
- 1 teaspoon baking powder
- 1 teaspoon ground cinnamon
- Pinch ground cloves
- Nonstick cooking spray

Directions:
1. Set the yogurt, eggs, and vanilla in a blender and pulse to combine.

2. Add the oats, sweetener, baking powder, cinnamon, and cloves to the blender and blend until the batter is smooth.
3. Set a large skillet and lightly coat it with cooking spray.
4. Spoon ¼ cup of batter per pancake, 4 at a time, into the skillet. Cook the pancakes until the bottoms are firm and golden, about 4 minutes.
5. Flip the pancakes over and cook the other side until they are cooked through, about 3 minutes.
6. Detach the pancakes to a plate and repeat with the remaining batter.
7. Serve with fresh fruit.

Nutrition:
Calories: 244
Fat: 8.1g
Fiber: 4.0g
Protein: 13.1g
Carbohydrates: 28.1g
Sugar: 3.0g
Sodium: 82mg

8. Apple and Pumpkin Waffles

Preparation Time: 10 minutes **Cooking Time:** 20 minutes **Servings:** 6

Ingredients:
- 2¼ cups whole-wheat pastry flour
- 2 tablespoons granulated sweetener
- 1 tablespoon baking powder
- 1 teaspoon ground cinnamon
- 1 teaspoon ground nutmeg
- 4 eggs
- 1¼ cups pure pumpkin purée
- 1 apple, peeled, cored, and finely chopped
- Melted coconut oil, for cooking

Directions:
1. In a large bowl, merge together the flour, sweetener, baking powder, cinnamon, and nutmeg.
2. In a small bowl, set together the eggs and pumpkin.
3. Attach the wet ingredients to the dry and whisk until smooth.
4. Stir the apple into the batter.
5. Cook the waffles based to the waffle maker manufacturer's directions, brushing your waffle iron with melted coconut oil, until all the batter is gone.
6. Serve immediately.

Nutrition:
Calories: 232
Fat: 4.1g
Protein: 10.9g
Carbohydrates: 40.1g
Fiber: 7.1g
Sugar: 5.1g
Sodium: 52mg

9. Buckwheat Crêpes

Preparation Time: 10 minutes **Cooking Time:** 20 minutes **Servings:** 5

Ingredients:
- 1½ cups skim milk
- 3 eggs
- 1 tsp. extra-virgin olive oil, plus more for the skillet
- 1 cup buckwheat flour
- ½ cup whole-wheat flour
- ½ cup 2 percent plain Greek yogurt
- 1 cup sliced strawberries
- 1 cup blueberries

Directions:
1. In a large bowl, merge together the milk, eggs, and 1 teaspoon of oil until well combined.
2. Into a medium bowl, sift together the buckwheat and whole-wheat flours. Attach the dry ingredients to the wet ingredients and whisk until well combined and very smooth.
3. Set the batter to rest for at least 2 hours before cooking.
4. Place a large skillet or crêpe pan over medium-high heat and lightly coat the bottom with oil.
5. Set about ¼ cup of batter into the skillet. Swirl the pan until the batter completely coats the bottom.
6. Cook the crêpe for about 1 minute, then flip it over. Cook the other side of the crêpe for another minute, until lightly browned. Transfer the cooked crêpe to a plate and cover with a clean dish towel to keep warm.
7. Redo until the batter is used up; you should have about 10 crêpes.
8. Spoon 1 tablespoon of yogurt onto each crêpe and place two crêpes on each plate.
9. Top with berries and serve.

Nutrition:
Calories: 330
Fat: 6.9g
Protein: 15.9g
Carbohydrates: 54.1g
Fiber: 7.9g
Sugar: 11.1g
Sodium: 100mg

10. Mushroom Frittata

Preparation Time: 10 minutes **Cooking Time:** 15 minutes **Servings:** 4

Ingredients:
- 8 large eggs
- ½ cup skim milk
- ¼ teaspoon ground nutmeg
- Sea salt and freshly ground black pepper
- 2 teaspoons extra-virgin olive oil
- 2 cups sliced wild mushrooms (cremini, oyster, shiitake, portobello, etc.)
- ½ red onion, chopped
- 1 teaspoon minced garlic
- ½ cup goat cheese, crumbled

Directions:
1. Preheat the broiler.
2. In a medium bowl, merge together the eggs, milk, and nutmeg until well combined. Flavor the egg mixture lightly with salt and pepper and set it aside.
3. Set an ovenproof skillet over medium heat and add the oil, coating the bottom completely by tilting the pan.
4. Sauté the mushrooms, onion, and garlic until translucent, about 7 minutes.
5. Pour the egg mixture into the skillet and cook until the bottom of the frittata is set, lifting the edges of the cooked egg to allow the uncooked egg to seep under.
6. Set the skillet to boil until the top is set about 1 minute.
7. Sprinkle the goat cheese on the frittata and broil until the cheese is melted, about 1 minute more.
8. Remove from the oven. Cut into 4 wedges to serve.

Nutrition:
Calories: 227
Fat: 15.1g
Protein: 17.1g
Carbohydrates: 5.1g
Fiber: 0.9g
Sugar: 4.1g
Sodium: 224mg

11. Tropical Yogurt Kiwi Bowl

Preparation Time: 5 minutes **Cooking Time:** 0 minutes **Servings:** 2

Ingredients:
- 1½ cups plain low-fat Greek yogurt
- 2 kiwis, peeled and sliced
- 2 tablespoons shredded unsweetened coconut flakes
- 2 tablespoons halved walnuts
- 1 tablespoon chia seeds
- 2 teaspoons honey, divided (optional)

Directions:
1. Divide the yogurt between two small bowls.
2. Top each serving of yogurt with half of the kiwi slices, coconut flakes, walnuts, chia seeds, and honey (if using).

Nutrition:
Calories: 261
Fat: 9.1g
Protein: 21.1g
Carbohydrates: 23.1g
Fiber: 6.1g
Sugar: 14.1g
Sodium: 84mg

12. Banana Crêpe Cakes

Preparation Time: 10 minutes **Cooking Time:** 0 minutes **Servings:** 1

Ingredients:
- Avocado oil cooking spray
- 4 ounces (113 g) reduced-fat plain cream cheese, softened
- 2 medium bananas
- 4 large eggs
- ½ teaspoon vanilla extract
- ⅛ teaspoon salt

Directions:
1. Heat a large skillet over low heat. Coat the cooking surface with cooking spray and allow the pan to heat for another 2 to 3 minutes.
2. Meanwhile, in a medium bowl, mash the cream cheese and bananas together with a fork until combined. The bananas can be a little chunky.
3. Set the eggs, vanilla, and salt, and mix well.
4. For each cake, drop 2 tablespoons of the batter onto the warmed skillet and use the bottom of a large spoon or ladle to spread it thin. Let it cook for 7 to minutes.
5. Flip the cake over and cook briefly, about 1 minute.

Nutrition:
Calories: 176 | Carbohydrates: 15.1g | Sodium: 214mg
Fat: 9.1g | Fiber: 2.1g
Protein: 9.1g | Sugar: 8.1g

13. Tacos with Pico De Gallo

Preparation Time: 10 minutes **Cooking Time:** 10 minutes **Servings:** 4

Ingredients:

For the Taco Filling:
- Avocado oil cooking spray
- 1 medium green bell pepper, chopped
- 8 large eggs
- ¼ cup shredded sharp Cheddar cheese
- 4 (6-inch) whole-wheat tortillas
- 1 cup fresh spinach leaves
- ½ cup Pico de Gallo
- Scallions, chopped, for garnish (optional)
- Avocado slices, for garnish (optional)

For the Pico De Gallo:
- 1 tomato, diced
- ½ large white onion, diced
- 2 tablespoons chopped fresh cilantro
- ½ jalapeño pepper, stemmed, seeded, and diced
- 1 tablespoon freshly squeezed lime juice
- ⅛ teaspoon salt

Directions:

To Make the Taco Filling
1. Heat a medium skillet over medium-low heat. When hot, coat the cooking surface with cooking spray and put the pepper in the skillet. Cook for 4 minutes.
2. Meanwhile, set the eggs in a medium bowl, then add the cheese and whisk to combine. Pour the eggs and cheese into the skillet with the green peppers and scramble until the eggs are fully cooked, about 5 minutes.
3. Microwave the tortillas very briefly, about 8 seconds.
4. For each serving, top a tortilla with one-quarter of the spinach, eggs, and pico de gallo. Garnish with scallions and avocado slices (if using).

To Make the Pico De Gallo
1. In a medium bowl, merge the tomato, onion, cilantro, pepper, lime juice, and salt. Mix well and serve.

Nutrition:
Calories: 277 | Carbohydrates: 28.1g | Sodium: 563mg
Fat: 12.1g | Fiber: 2.9g
Protein: 16.1g | Sugar: 8.1g

14. Portobello and Chicken Sausage Frittata

Preparation Time: 10 minutes **Cooking Time:** 15 minutes **Servings:** 4

Ingredients:
- Avocado oil cooking spray
- 1 cup roughly chopped portobello mushrooms
- 1 medium green bell pepper, diced
- 1 medium red bell pepper, diced
- 8 large eggs
- ¾ cup half-and-half
- ¼ cup unsweetened almond milk
- 6 links maple-flavored chicken or turkey breakfast sausage, cut into ¼-inch pieces

Directions:
1. Preheat the oven to 375F (190C).
2. Warmth a large, oven-safe skillet over medium-low heat. When hot, coat the cooking surface with cooking spray.
3. Heat the mushrooms, green bell pepper, and red bell pepper in the skillet. Cook for 5 minutes.
4. Meanwhile, in a medium bowl, set the eggs, half-and-half, and almond milk.
5. Add the sausage to the skillet and cook for 2 minutes.
6. Set the egg mixture into the skillet, then transfer the skillet from the stove to the oven and set to bake for 15 minutes until the middle is firm and spongy.

Nutrition:
Calories: 281 | Carbohydrates: 10.1g | Sodium: 445mg
Fat: 17.1g | Fiber: 2.1g
Protein: 20.9g | Sugar: 7.1g

15. Egg Salad Sandwiches

Preparation Time: 10 minutes
Cooking Time: 0 minutes
Servings: 4

Ingredients:
- 8 large hardboiled eggs
- 3 tablespoons plain low-fat Greek yogurt
- 1 tablespoon mustard
- ½ teaspoon freshly ground black pepper
- 1 teaspoon chopped fresh chives
- 4 slices 100% whole-wheat bread
- 2 cups fresh spinach, loosely packed

Directions:
1. Skin the eggs and cut them in half.
2. In a large bowl, mash the eggs with a fork, leaving chunks.
3. Add the yogurt, mustard, pepper, and chives, and mix.
4. For each portion, layer 1 slice of bread with one quarter of the egg salad and spinach.

Nutrition:
Calories: 278
Fat: 12.1g
Protein: 20.1g
Carbohydrates: 23.1g
Fiber: 2.9g
Sugar: 3.1g
Sodium: 365mg

16. Shrimp with Scallion Grits

Preparation Time: 10 minutes
Cooking Time: 20 minutes
Servings: 6-8

Ingredients:
- 1½ cups fat-free milk
- 1½ cups water
- 2 bay leaves
- 1 cup stone-ground corn grits
- ¼ cup seafood broth
- 2 garlic cloves, diced
- 2 scallions, white and green parts, thinly diced
- 1 pound (454 g) medium shrimp, shelled and deveined
- ½ teaspoon dried dill
- ½ teaspoon smoked paprika
- ¼ teaspoon celery seeds

Directions:
1. In a medium stockpot, merge the milk, water, and bay leaves and bring to a boil over high heat.
2. Gradually put in the grits, stirring continuously.
3. Set the heat to low, cover, and cook for 5 to 7 minutes, stirring often until the grits are soft and tender. Detach from the heat and discard the bay leaves.
4. In a skillet, bring the broth to boil over medium heat.
5. Attach the garlic and scallions, and sauté for 3 to minutes until softened.
6. Attach the shrimp, dill, paprika, and celery seeds and cook for about 7 minutes until the shrimp is light pink but not overcooked.
7. Set each dish with ¼ cup of grits, topped with shrimp.

Nutrition:
Calories: 198
Fat: 1.0g
Protein: 20.1g
Carbohydrates: 24.9g
Fiber: 1.0g
Sugar: 3.1g
Sodium: 204mg

17. Breakfast Cheddar Zucchini Casserole

Preparation Time: 10 minutes
Cooking Time: 35 minutes
Servings: 12-15

Ingredients:
- Nonstick cooking spray
- 6 medium brown eggs
- 8 medium egg whites
- 1 green bell pepper, chopped
- ½ small yellow onion, chopped
- 1 zucchini, finely grated, with water pressed out
- 1 cup shredded reduced-fat Cheddar cheese
- 1 teaspoon paprika
- ½ teaspoon garlic powder

Directions:
1. Preheat the oven to 350F (180C). Set a large cast iron skillet with cooking spray.
2. In a medium bowl, whisk the eggs and egg whites together.
3. Add the bell pepper, onion, zucchini, cheese, paprika, and garlic powder, mix well, and pour into the prepared skillet.

4. Bring the skillet to the oven and bake for 35 minutes. Remove from the oven and let rest for 5 minutes before serving with Broccoli Stalk Slaw.

Nutrition:

Calories: 79　　Carbohydrates: 2.1g　　Sodium: 133mg
Fat: 4.1g　　Fiber: 1.1g
Protein: 8.1g　　Sugar: 1.2g

18. Banana and Zucchini Bread

Preparation Time: 15 minutes　　**Cooking Time:** 45 minutes　　**Servings:** 4

Ingredients:

- 1½ cups gluten-free all-purpose flour
- 1 cup almond meal
- ½ cup chickpea flour
- 1 teaspoon salt
- 1 teaspoon baking powder
- 1 teaspoon baking soda
- ½ teaspoon ground nutmeg
- ½ teaspoon ground cinnamon
- 3 medium brown eggs
- ¼ cup sunflower seed oil
- 2 ripe bananas, mashed
- 2 zucchinis, grated, with water squeezed out
- 2 teaspoons almond extract

Directions:

1. Preheat the oven to 350F (180C). Line a baking pan with parchment paper.
2. In a large bowl, merge the gluten-free flour, almond meal, chickpea flour, salt, baking powder, baking soda, nutmeg, and cinnamon.
3. In a separate large bowl, set the eggs, oil, bananas, zucchini, and almond extract together well.
4. Set the dry ingredients into the wet ingredients, stir until well combined, and pour into the prepared pan.
5. Bring the pan to the oven and bake for 40 to 45 minutes until a butter knife inserted into the center comes out clean. Remove from the oven and let the bread rest for 15 minutes before serving.

Nutrition:

Calories: 204　　Carbohydrates: 21.1g　　Sodium: 324mg
Fat: 11.1g　　Fiber: 4.1g
Protein: 6.1g　　Sugar: 4.1g

19. Breakfast Grain Porridge

Preparation Time: 5 minutes　　**Cooking Time:** 35 minutes　　**Servings:** 8

Ingredients:

- 1 cup teff
- 1 cup stone-ground corn grits
- 1 cup quinoa
- ¼ teaspoon whole cloves
- 1 tablespoon sunflower seed oil
- 5 cups water
- 2 cups roughly chopped fresh fruit
- 2 cups unsalted crushed nuts

Directions:

1. In an electric pressure cooker, combine the teff, grits, quinoa, and cloves.
2. Add the oil and water, mixing with a fork.
3. Choose the Porridge setting and cook for 20 minutes.
4. Once cooking is complete, allow the pressure to release naturally. Carefully remove the lid.
5. Serve each portion with ¼ cup fresh fruit and ¼ cup nuts of your choice.

Nutrition:

Calories: 418　　Carbohydrates: 49.1g　　Sodium: 6mg
Fat: 19.1g　　Fiber: 9.1g
Protein: 13.2g　　Sugar: 5.1g

20. Tomato Waffles

Preparation Time: 15 minutes　　**Cooking Time:** 40 minutes　　**Servings:** 8

Ingredients:

- 2 cups low-fat buttermilk
- ½ cup crushed tomato
- 1 medium egg
- 2 medium egg whites
- 1 cup gluten-free all-purpose flour
- ½ cup almond flour
- ½ cup coconut flour
- 2 teaspoons baking powder

- ½ teaspoon baking soda
- ½ teaspoon dried chives
- Nonstick cooking spray

Directions:
1. Heat a waffle iron.
2. In a medium bowl, whisk the buttermilk, tomato, egg, and egg whites together.
3. In another bowl, whisk the all-purpose flour, almond flour, coconut flour, baking powder, baking soda, and chives together.
4. Put in the wet ingredients to the dry ingredients.
5. Lightly spray the waffle iron with cooking spray.
6. Gently pour ¼- to ½-cup portions of batter into the waffle iron. Cook time for waffles will vary depending on the kind of waffle iron you use, but is usually 5 minutes per waffle. (Note: Once the waffle iron is hot, the cooking process is a bit faster. Repeat until no batter remains.
7. Enjoy the waffles warm with Dandelion Greens with Sweet Onion.

Nutrition:
Calories: 144
Fat: 4.1g
Protein: 7.1g
Carbohydrates: 21.2g
Fiber: 5.1g
Sugar: 2.9g
Sodium: 171mg

Lunch

21. Green Salad with Berries and Sweet Potatoes

Preparation Time: 15 minutes **Cooking Time:** 20 minutes **Servings:** 4

Ingredients:

For the vinaigrette
- 1-pint blackberries
- 2 tablespoons red wine vinegar
- 1 tablespoon honey

For the salad
- 1 sweet potato, cubed
- 1 teaspoon extra-virgin olive oil
- 8 cups salad greens (baby spinach, spicy greens, romaine)
- 3 tablespoons extra-virgin olive oil
- ¼ teaspoon salt
- Freshly ground black pepper
- ½ red onion, sliced
- ¼ cup crumbled goat cheese

Directions:

For vinaigrette
1. In a blender jar, combine the blackberries, vinegar, honey, oil, salt, and pepper, and process until smooth. Set aside.

For salad

1. Preheat the oven to 425F. Line a baking sheet with parchment paper.
2. Mix the sweet potato with the olive oil. Bring to the prepared baking sheet and roast, stirring once halfway through, until tender. Remove and cool for a few minutes.
3. In a large bowl, set the greens with the red onion and cooled sweet potato, and drizzle with the vinaigrette. Serve topped with 1 tablespoon of goat cheese per serving.

Nutrition:
Calories: 168
Fat: 1.1g
Protein: 6.2g
Carbohydrates: 33.8g
Fiber: 1.1g
Sugar: 2.8g
Sodium: 33mg

22. Three Bean and Scallion Salad

Preparation Time: 10 minutes **Cooking Time:** 0 minute **Servings:** 8

Ingredients:
- 1 (15-ounce) can low-sodium chickpeas
- 1 (15-ounce) can low-sodium kidney beans
- 1 (15-ounce) can low-sodium white beans
- 1 red bell pepper
- ¼ cup chopped scallions
- ¼ cup finely chopped fresh basil
- 3 garlic cloves, minced
- 2 tablespoons extra-virgin olive oil
- 1 tablespoon red wine vinegar
- 1 teaspoon Dijon mustard
- ¼ teaspoon freshly ground black pepper

Directions:
1. Toss chickpeas, kidney beans, white beans, bell pepper, scallions, basil, and garlic gently.
2. Blend together olive oil, vinegar, mustard, and pepper. Toss with the salad.
3. Wrap and chill for 1 hour.

Nutrition:
Calories: 183
Fat: 12.1g
Protein: 8.1g
Carbohydrates: 11.1g
Fiber: 2.9g
Sugar: 5.9g
Sodium: 850mg

23. Rainbow Bean Salad

Preparation Time: 15 minutes **Cooking Time:** 0 minute **Servings:** 5

Ingredients:
- 1 (15-ounce) can low-sodium black beans
- 1 avocado, diced
- 1 cup cherry
- 3 tomatoes, halved
- 1 cup chopped baby spinach
- ½ cup red bell pepper
- ¼ cup jicama
- ½ cup scallions
- ¼ cup fresh cilantro
- 2 tablespoons lime juice
- 1 tablespoon extra-virgin olive oil
- 2 garlic cloves, minced
- 1 teaspoon honey
- ¼ teaspoon salt
- ¼ teaspoon freshly ground black pepper

Directions:
1. Mix black beans, avocado, tomatoes, spinach, bell pepper, jicama, scallions, and cilantro.
2. Blend lime juice, oil, garlic, honey, salt, and pepper. Add to the salad and toss.
3. Chill for 1 hour before serving.

Nutrition:
Calories: 244
Fat: 8.1g
Protein: 13.1g
Carbohydrates: 28.1g
Fiber: 4.0g
Sugar: 3.0g
Sodium: 82mg

24. Warm Barley and Squash Salad

Preparation Time: 20 minutes **Cooking Time:** 40 minutes **Servings:** 8

Ingredients:
- 1 small butternut squash
- 3 tablespoons extra-virgin olive oil
- 2 cups broccoli florets
- 1 cup pearl barley

- 1 cup toasted chopped walnuts
- 2 cups baby kale - ½ red onion, sliced
- 2 tablespoons balsamic vinegar
- 2 garlic cloves, minced
- ½ teaspoon salt
- ¼ teaspoon black pepper

Directions:
1. Preheat the oven to 400F. Line a baking sheet with parchment paper.
2. Peel off the squash, and slice into dice. In a large bowl, toss the squash with 2 teaspoons of olive oil. Set to the prepared baking sheet and roast for 20 minutes.
3. While the squash is roasting, toss the broccoli in the same bowl with 1 teaspoon of olive oil. After 20 minutes, flip the squash and push it to one side of the baking sheet. Attach the broccoli to the other side and continue to roast for 20 more minutes until tender.
4. While the veggies are roasting, in a pot, cover the barley with several inches of water. Boil, then adjust heat, cover, and simmer for 30 minutes until tender. Drain and rinse.
5. Transfer the barley to a large bowl, and toss with the cooked squash and broccoli, walnuts, kale, and onion.
6. In a small bowl, merge the remaining 2 tablespoons of olive oil, balsamic vinegar, garlic, salt, and pepper. Drizzle dressing over the salad and toss.

Nutrition:
Calories: 176
Fat: 9.1g
Protein: 9.1g
Carbohydrates: 15.1g
Fiber: 2.1g
Sugar: 8.1g
Sodium: 214mg

25. Citrus and Chicken Salad

Preparation Time: 10 minutes **Cooking Time:** 0 minute **Servings:** 4

Ingredients:
- 4 cups baby spinach
- 2 tablespoons extra-virgin olive oil
- 1 tablespoon lemon juice
- ⅛ teaspoon salt
- 2 cups chopped cooked chicken
- 2 mandarin oranges
- ½ peeled grapefruit, sectioned
- ¼ cup sliced almonds

Directions:
1. Toss spinach with the olive oil, lemon juice, salt, and pepper.
2. Add the chicken, oranges, grapefruit, and almonds to the bowl. Toss gently.
3. Arrange on 4 plates and serve.

Nutrition:
Calories: 157
Protein: 5.4g
Carbohydrates: 26.2g
Dietary Fiber: 6.6g
Sugars: 2.2g
Fat: 4.7g

26. Blueberry and Chicken Salad

Preparation Time: 10 minutes **Cooking Time:** 0 minute **Servings:** 4

Ingredients:
- 2 cups chopped cooked chicken
- 1 cup fresh blueberries
- ¼ cup almonds
- 1 celery stalk
- ¼ cup red onion
- 1 tablespoon fresh basil
- 1 tablespoon fresh cilantro
- ½ cup plain, vegan mayonnaise
- ¼ teaspoon salt
- ¼ teaspoon freshly ground black pepper
- 8 cups salad greens

Directions:
1. Toss chicken, blueberries, almonds, celery, onion, basil, and cilantro.
2. Blend yogurt, salt, and pepper. Stir chicken salad to combine.
3. Situate 2 cups of salad greens on each of 4 plates and divide the chicken salad among the plates to serve.

Nutrition:
Calories: 265
Fat: 3.1g
Protein: 7.9g
Carbohydrates: 50.9g
Fiber: 7.1g
Sugar: 0.5g
Sodium: 141mg

27. Joseph's Bacon

Preparation Time: 10 minutes   **Cooking Time:** 15 minutes   **Servings:** 6

Ingredients:
- 1 (16 ounces) package of thick-cut bacon

Directions:
1. Set a large baking sheet with 2 sheets of aluminum foil, ensuring the pan is completely covered.
2. Pile the bacon strips on the prepared baking sheet, keeping at least ½-inch space between strips.
3. Set a pan in the cold oven. Heat oven to 425 degrees F
4. Cook bacon for 14 minutes.
5. Place cooked bacon on a paper towel.
6. Let warm for 5 minutes for bacon to firm.
7. Serve and enjoy!

Nutrition:
Calories: 91　　Carbohydrates: 0.1g　　Sodium: 155mg
Fat: 4.8g　　Fiber: 0.1g
Protein: 11.2g　　Sugar: 0g

28. Texas Goulash

Preparation Time: 25 minutes   **Cooking Time:** 60 minutes   **Servings:** 6

Ingredients:
- 2 tablespoons of water
- 3 teaspoons of chili powder, or to taste
- 2 teaspoons of white sugar replacement (like stevia)
- ¼ teaspoon of salt
- ¼ teaspoon of ground black pepper
- 1 (8 ounces) package of dry elbow macaroni
- 1 pound of ground beef
- ¼ cup of bell pepper green, hashed
- ¼ cup of chopped onion
- 1-½ cups of canned pinto beans, rinsed and drained
- ¾ cup of tomato paste
- 2 cups of water

Directions:
1. Cook and whisk ground beef, bell pepper, and onion in a large pot over medium-high heat until beef is ready and vegetables are tender, 5 to 7 minutes.
2. Spill pinto beans into a saucepan and cook over medium heat until heated for about 5 minutes. Stir in tomato paste.
3. Combine 2 cups plus 2 tablespoons of water, salt, chili powder, sugar, and pepper in a small bowl.
4. Whisk into the beef mixture. Attach pinto bean mixture. Secure and parboil for 20 minutes.
5. While goulash cooks, set a large pot of lightly salted water to a boil. Cook elbow macaroni in the boiling water, occasionally stirring, until tender yet firm to the bite, about 8 minutes. Drain.
6. Mix cooked macaroni into the goulash, cover.
7. Simmer for 30 minutes to 1 hour.
8. Serve and enjoy!

Nutrition:
Calories: 68　　Carbohydrates: 2.9g　　Sodium: 126mg
Fat: 4.1g　　Fiber: 1.1g
Protein: 6.2g　　Sugar: 2.0g

29. Roasted Chickpea

Preparation Time: 10 minutes   **Cooking Time:** 40 minutes   **Servings:** 4

Ingredients:
- ¼ tsp. of salt to taste
- ground black pepper to taste
- 1 (15 ounces) can of garbanzo beans, drained and rinsed
- 2 teaspoons of olive oil

Directions:
1. Preheat oven to 425F.
2. Set garbanzo beans in a baking dish and pat dry with a paper towel.
3. Bake in the warmth oven, stirring halfway through, for about 22 minutes. Whisk with olive oil, salt, and pepper in a bowl.
4. Bring to the baking dish.
5. Continue baking chickpeas, stirring halfway through, until ready and dry outside, about 22 minutes more.
6. Serve and enjoy!

Nutrition:

Calories: 168	Carbohydrates: 33.8g	Sodium: 33mg
Fat: 1.1g	Fiber: 1.1g	
Protein: 6.2g	Sugar: 2.8g	

30. Coconut Meringue Cake

Preparation Time: 20 minutes **Cooking Time:** 30 minutes **Servings:** 9

Ingredients:
- 1 teaspoon of vanilla extract
- 3 egg whites
- 1 tablespoon of white sugar replacement (like stevia)
- 1-½ cups of flaked coconut
- ½ cup of butter, softened
- 1 teaspoon of white sugar replacement (like stevia)
- 3 egg yolks
- 1 cup of all-purpose flour
- 1-½ teaspoons of baking powder
- ¼ teaspoon of salt
- ⅓ cup of milk

Directions:
1. Preheat oven to 350F.
2. Grease a 9x9-inch baking pan. Beat butter and 1 tablespoon white sugar until light and fluffy. Beat in egg yolks.
3. Combine flour, baking powder, and salt in a bowl.
4. Attach flour mixture to butter mixture in two parts, alternating with milk and vanilla, beginning and ending with flour mixture.
5. Spread in the prepared pan.
6. For the topping, set the egg whites until soft peaks form. Add 1 teaspoon of the white sugar gradually and beat until egg whites are stiff.
7. Fold in the coconut.
8. Bake in warmth oven until meringue topping starts to brown and a toothpick inserted in the center comes out clean, for about 30 to 35 minutes.

Nutrition:

Calories: 190	Carbohydrates: 31.9g	Sodium: 112mg
Fat: 4.9g	Fiber: 2.9g	
Protein: 5.1g	Sugar: 6.0g	

31. Banana Nut Bread

Preparation Time: 25 minutes **Cooking Time:** 75 minutes **Servings:** 10

Ingredients:
- 1-½ teaspoons of baking powder
- ½ teaspoon of baking soda
- 1 cup of chopped walnuts
- 2 ripe bananas, mashed
- 1 package of cream cheese, softened
- 1 teaspoon of white sugar replacement (like stevia)
- ½ cup of butter
- 2 eggs, well-beaten
- 2-¼ cups of all-purpose flour

Directions:
1. Preheat an oven to 350F.
2. Grease a 9x5-inch loaf pan.
3. Beat together the cream cheese, eggs, sugar, butter, and banana in a large bowl until smooth.
4. Spill in the flour, baking soda, baking powder, and walnuts until just combined.
5. Spill the batter into the prepared loaf pan.
6. Bake in the warmth oven until a toothpick inserted into the center comes out clean, about 1 hour and 15 minutes.
7. Serve and enjoy!

Nutrition:

Calories: 321	Carbohydrates: 49.3g	Cholesterol: 81.8mg
Protein: 7.8g	Fat: 25.9g	

32. Oyster Stew

Preparation Time: 15 minutes **Cooking Time:** 20 minutes **Servings:** 6

Ingredients:
- 2 pints of half-and-half
- 1 teaspoon of dried parsley
- salt and ground black pepper to taste
- 1 (12 ounces) can think of oysters
- 2 dashes of Louisiana-style hot sauce
- ¼ cup of butter
- 1 cup of finely chopped celery
- ½ cup of chopped green onion

- ½ cup of hashed red bell pepper

Directions:
1. Dissolve the butter in a saucepan over medium heat until it begins to foam.
2. Cook and stir the onion, celery, and red bell pepper in the hot butter until soft, about 8 to 10 minutes.
3. Attach the parsley and season with salt and black pepper.
4. Continue cooking until the mixture begins to bubble. Attach the oysters and any liquid from the can lead to the stew along with the Louisiana-style hot sauce.
5. Set the mixture to a simmer and cook until the oysters begin to curl, 10 to 15 minutes.
6. Detach the saucepan from heat and allow the stew to sit 5 minutes before serving.

Nutrition:
Calories: 53
Protein: 9.2g
Carbohydrates: 11.8g
Fat: 30.3g
Cholesterol: 114.2mg

33. Pecan-Oatmeal Pancakes

Preparation Time: 10 minutes **Cooking Time:** 15 minutes **Servings:** 6

Ingredients:
- 1 cup quick cooking oats
- 1½ teaspoons baking powder
- 2 eggs
- ⅓ cup mashed banana
- ⅓ cup skim milk
- ½ teaspoon vanilla extract
- 2 tablespoons chopped pecans
- 1 tablespoon canola oil

Directions:
1. Press the oats in a food processor until they are ground into a powder-like consistency.
2. Transfer the ground oats to a small bowl, along with the baking powder. Mix well.
3. Whisk together the eggs, mashed banana, skim milk, and vanilla in another bowl. Spill into the bowl of dry ingredients and stir with a spatula just until well incorporated. Add the chopped pecans and mix well.
4. In a large nonstick skillet, warmth the canola oil over medium heat.
5. Spoon ¼ cup of batter for each pancake onto the hot skillet, swirling the pan so the batter covers the bottom evenly. Cook until bubbles set on top of the pancake. Flip the pancake and cook for an additional 1 to 2 minutes, or until the pancake is browned and cooked through. Repeat with the remaining batter.
6. Remove from the heat and serve on a plate.

Nutrition:
Calories: 131
Fat: 6.9g
Protein: 5.2g
Carbohydrates: 13.1g
Fiber: 2.0g
Sugar: 2.9g
Sodium: 120mg

34. Basic Bread Stuffing

Preparation Time: 40 minutes **Cooking Time:** 10 minutes **Servings:** 12

Ingredients:
- 6 cups of diced whole-grain bread
- 1 tablespoon of paprika
- ¼ cup of egg substitute
- 2-½ cups of low fat, low sodium chicken broth
- 3 onions, diced
- salt and pepper to flavor

Directions:
1. In a skillet over medium-high warmth, heat ½ cup of the chicken broth.
2. Attach onions and cook for 10 minutes until softened.
3. Combine the remaining broth, cooked onions, bread, egg replacer, paprika, salt, and pepper in a bowl. Stir
4. Set mixture inside the cavity of a turkey.
5. If stuffing is to be baked separately from the turkey, set stuffing in a preheated 350-degree oven and bake for 45 minutes. Serve.

Nutrition:
Calories: 67
Protein: 3.9g
Carbohydrates: 10.7g
Fat: 1.1g
Cholesterol: 0.1mg

35. Dill Pickle Dip

Preparation Time: 10 minutes **Cooking Time:** 15 minutes **Servings:** 12

Ingredients:

- 2 tablespoons of pickle juice, or more to taste
- 1 teaspoon of dried dill weed
- ½ teaspoon of kosher salt
- 1 pinch of ground black pepper
- 1 (8 ounces) package of cream cheese, at room temperature
- 1 cup of chopped dill pickles, or more to taste
- ¼ cup of chopped sweet onion

Directions:
1. Spill cream cheese in a bowl with a wooden spoon until smooth.
2. Stir in dill pickles, onion, pickle juice, dill weed, salt, and pepper until evenly distributed.
3. Refrigerate before serving, at least 1 hour.

Nutrition:
Calories: 79　　Carbohydrates: 2.4g　　Cholesterol: 20.5mg
Protein: 2.5g　　Fat: 5.5g

36. Funnel Cakes

Preparation Time: 15 minutes　　**Cooking Time:** 10 minutes　　**Servings:** 4

Ingredients:
- 1 tablespoon of baking powder
- 1 teaspoon of vanilla extract
- ½ teaspoon of salt
- ¼ cup of vegetable oil for frying or as needed
- 1-¼ cups of all-purpose flour, or more if needed
- 1 teaspoon of white sugar replacement (like stevia)
- ½ cup of water
- ½ cup of milk
- 1 egg

Directions:
1. Pour oil into a frying pan.
2. Heat over medium-high heat.
3. Mix sugar, flour, water, egg, milk, baking powder, vanilla extract and salt in a blender until smooth.
4. Attach more flour if the batter is too watery.
5. Place your finger over the hole in a funnel and fill the funnel with the batter.
6. Place the filled funnel on top of the pan, release your finger.
7. Swirl batter in hot oil; cook until golden brown, about 4 to 5 minutes per side. Serve.

Nutrition:
Calories: 56　　Carbohydrates: 46.1g　　Cholesterol: 48.9mg
Protein: 8.6g　　Fat: 2.5g

37. Shrimp Burgers

Preparation Time: 35 minutes　　**Cooking Time:** 10 minutes　　**Servings:** 3

Ingredients:
- 1 teaspoon of seafood seasoning (such as Old Bay®)
- ground black pepper to taste
- 2 tablespoons of frozen butter cut into small pieces
- 2 tablespoons of canola oil, or as needed
- ¾ pound of raw, peeled shrimp
- 1 egg, beaten
- ¼ cup of breadcrumbs
- 1 small lemon, juiced
- 1 tablespoon of lemon zest

Directions:
1. Set to chop 3 or 4 shrimp and place in a bowl.
2. Pulse remaining shrimp in a food processor and transfer them to the bowl with the sliced shrimp.
3. Combine egg, breadcrumbs, lemon juice, lemon zest, seafood seasoning, and black pepper in a bowl.
4. Add shrimp and butter. Form mixture into three patties and refrigerate for at least 30 minutes.
5. Warmth oil in a skillet over medium heat.
6. Cook patties until browned, 4 to 5 minutes.

Nutrition:
Calories: 89　　Carbohydrates: 6.4g　　Cholesterol: 254.6mg
Protein: 21g　　Fat: 20.1g

38. Whole Wheat Chapatti

Preparation Time: 10 minutes　　**Cooking Time:** 2 minutes　　**Servings:** 4

Ingredients:
- 1 tablespoon of olive oil
- ¼ cup of water
- 1 cup of whole wheat flour
- 1 pinch of salt

Directions:
1. Spill together the flour and salt in a bowl.
2. Whisk in olive oil and water, and then knead until firm and elastic.
3. Set into four balls and roll as flat as possible with a rolling pin.
4. Heat a frying pan over medium-high heat.
5. Cook the chapatti on both sides until golden brown.
6. If desired, drizzle with additional olive oil before serving. Serve and enjoy!

Nutrition:
Calories: 123
Protein: 3.1g
Carbohydrates: 22.8g
Fat: 2.9g

39. Sugar Free Strawberry Cheesecake

Preparation Time: 10 minutes **Cooking Time:** 60 minutes **Servings:** 1

Ingredients:
- 1 package of cream cheese, softened
- 1-½ cups of milk
- 1 (1 ounce) package of cheesecake flavor sugar-free instant pudding mix
- 2 pints of fresh strawberries, sliced
- ¾ cup of graham cracker crumbs
- 3 tablespoons of butter, melted
- ¼ teaspoon of ground cinnamon
- ¼ teaspoon of ground nutmeg

Directions:
1. Mix graham cracker crumbs, cinnamon, melted butter and nutmeg in a bowl.
2. Press the mixture into a cake pan. Refrigerate while you prepare the filling.
3. Merge the cream cheese in a bowl with an electric mixer on medium speed until softened.
4. Set the speed to low, and gradually attach the milk, a little at a time (the mixture will be watery).
5. Beat in pudding mix until filling is thick and smooth.
6. Spread half of the cream cheese filling into the bottom of the graham cracker crust.
7. Spread half of the strawberries on top of the filling.
8. Repeat cheesecake layer and strawberry layer.
9. Chill the pie in the refrigerator until cold, at least hour. Serve and enjoy!

Nutrition:
Calories: 269
Protein: 5.4g
Carbohydrates: 24.2g
Fat: 16.4g
Cholesterol: 58.2mg

40. Shrimps Saganaki

Preparation Time: 10 minutes **Cooking Time:** 35 minutes **Servings:** 4

Ingredients:
- 1 can of diced tomatoes, drained
- ¼ teaspoon of garlic powder (Optional)
- ¼ cup of olive oil
- 1 (8 ounces) package of feta cheese, cubed
- 1 pound of medium shrimp, with shells
- 1 onion, chopped
- 2 tablespoons of chopped fresh parsley
- 1 cup of white wine
- 1 pinch of salt and pepper to flavor

Directions:
1. Set about 2 inches of water to a boil in a large saucepan.
2. Attach the shrimp; the water should just cover them.
3. Boil for 5 minutes, then drain, keeping the liquid, and set aside.
4. Heat about 2 tbsp. of oil in a saucepan.
5. Attach the onions; cook and stir until the onions are soft.
6. Merge in the parsley, wine, tomatoes, garlic powder, and remaining olive oil.
7. Simmer, occasionally stirring, for about 30 minutes.
8. While the sauce is broiling, the shrimps should have become cool enough to handle.
9. First, detach the legs, and then pull off the shells parting the head and tail.
10. When the sauce is thickened, spill in the shrimp stock and shrimp. Bring to a parboil and cook for about minutes.
11. Attach the feta cheese and remove it from the heat. Let stand until the cheese starts to dissolve.
12. Serve warm and enjoy!

Nutrition:
Calories: 357
Protein: 24.8g
Carbohydrates: 11.1g
Fat: 19.6g
Cholesterol: 223.1mg

Dinner

41. Cilantro and Lime Broccoli Rice

Preparation Time: 5 minutes 0 **Cooking Time:** 8 minutes **Servings:** 2

Ingredients:
- 2 ounces broccoli florets, finely chopped
- 2 green onions, white and green part separated
- 2 tablespoons chopped cilantro

Extra:
- ¼ teaspoon cayenne pepper
- ½ teaspoon garlic powder
- ½ cup of boiled brown rice
- 1 teaspoon lime juice
- 1 tablespoon olive oil

Directions:
1. Take a medium skillet pan, set it over medium heat, add oil and when hot, add white parts of green onion and then cook for 1 to 2 minutes until softened.
2. Stir in garlic, add broccoli, stir until mixed, then cover the pan and cook for 4 to 5 minutes until broccoli has turned slightly soft.
3. Add lime juice and cilantro, sprinkle with cayenne pepper, and then cook for 30 seconds.
4. Taste to adjust seasoning and then serve.

Nutrition:
Calories: 241 Carbohydrates: 28.7g Cholesterol: 23.4mg
Protein: 4.4g Fat: 8.8g

42. Spicy Garlic Pasta

Preparation Time: 5 minutes **Cooking Time:** 5 minutes **Servings:** 2

Ingredients:
- 2 ounces fettuccine pasta, boiled
- 1 tablespoon minced garlic
- ½ teaspoon red chili flakes
- 1 teaspoon lime juice
- 1 ½ tablespoon olive oil

Directions:
1. Take a medium skillet pan, place it over medium heat, add oil and when hot, add garlic and then cook for 1 minute until golden.
2. Stir in chili flakes, cook for 20 seconds, then add pasta and toss to coat.
3. Drizzle lime juice over pasta, cook for 1 minute until hot, and then serve.

Nutrition:
Calories: 310 Carbohydrates: 30.4g Cholesterol: 280.4mg
Protein: 45.6g Fat: 57.1g

43. Simple Beef Roast

Preparation Time: 10 minutes **Cooking Time:** 8 hours **Servings:** 8

Ingredients:
- 5 pounds' beef roast
- 2 tablespoons Italian seasoning
- 1 cup beef stock
- 1 tablespoon sweet paprika
- 3 tablespoons olive oil

Directions:
1. In your slow cooker, mix all the ingredients, cover and cook on low for 8 hours.
2. Carve the roast, divide it between plates and serve.

Nutrition:
Calories: 187 Fiber: 0.3 Protein: 86.5
Fat: 24.1, Carbohydrates: 0.9

44. Honey Garlic Butter Roasted Carrots

Preparation Time: 5 minutes **Cooking Time:** 20 minutes **Servings:** 2

Ingredients:
- 2 carrots
- ½ tablespoon minced garlic
- ⅛ teaspoon salt

Extra:
- ⅛ teaspoon ground black pepper
- ⅔ tablespoon honey
- 1 tablespoon chopped cilantro
- 1⅔ tablespoon butter, unsalted

Directions:
1. Switch on the oven, then set it to 425 F and let it preheat.
2. Meanwhile, prepare the carrot, and for this, peel them and diagonally cut them into 2-inch pieces.
3. Take a medium skillet pan, place it over medium heat, add butter and when it melts, add garlic and then cook for 1 minute until golden.
4. Remove pan from heat, add honey into the pan and then stir until well combined.
5. Add carrots into the pan, season with salt and black pepper and mix until well coated.
6. Set carrots in a single layer on a baking sheet greased with oil and then bake for 15 to 18 minutes until carrots have become tender and golden brown.

Nutrition:
Calories: 53 Carbohydrates: 11.8g Cholesterol: 114.2mg
Protein: 9.2g Fat: 30.3g

45. Colorful vegetable casserole

Preparation Time: 20 minutes **Cooking Time:** 1 hour 20 minutes **Servings:** 2

Ingredients:
- 1 organic zucchini
- 300 g of potatoes
- 1 onion, red
- 2 organic beefsteak tomatoes
- olive oil, as needed
- Sea salt and black pepper and thyme, fresh

- 100 g of feta
- 30 g of pitted olives
- Herbs for garnish, e.g., B. parsley, chives

Directions:
1. Wash zucchini and detach the ends, cut into cubes. Peel and wash the potatoes and divide into bite-sized pieces. Peel the onions and cut into slices. Wash tomatoes remove greens and cut into large cubes.
2. Warmth a pan with oil and fry the potatoes with the zucchini and onion. Pre heat the oven to 180F.
3. Wash and dry the thyme, pick off the leaves. Mix the tomatoes and 1 tbsp. thyme, flavor them well with sea salt and pepper. Put everything in a lightly greased casserole dish, cover with baking paper or aluminum foil and cook for about 50-60 minutes.
4. In the meantime, crumble the feta, cut the olives into rings and distribute them evenly on the casserole. Then cook for another 20 minutes.
5. Wash, dry and chop the herbs and finally garnish the casserole with the herbs.

Nutrition:
Calories: 167
Protein: 6.92 g
Fat: 6.85 g
Carbohydrates: 21.35 g

46. Lentil snack with tomato salsa

Preparation Time: 10 minutes **Cooking Time:** 45 minutes **Servings:** 2

Ingredients:
- 100 g of red lentils
- 1 small onion, red
- 80 g of wheat semolina
- 3 tbsp. paprika tomato paste
- 2 tbsp. mixed, chopped herbs (e.g., parsley, chervil, chives) - ½ organic lemon
- Sea salt and black pepper
- 1 organic tomato
- ½ red chili pepper, small
- 1 spring onion
- Olive oil, as needed
- 1 teaspoon rice syrup or maple syrup

Directions:
1. Cook the lentils based to the package instructions. Skin the onion and cut into small cubes. Mix the semolina with the finished lentils and leave to swell (about 3 minutes).
2. In the meantime, wash, dry and chop herbs. Add onion, paprika tomato paste (if you like) and herbs, stir and season with lemon juice, sea salt and pepper, then let cool.
3. For the tomato salsa, wash the tomatoes, remove the greens and cut into small cubes. Wash the chili peppers, cut lengthways, remove the seeds and partitions, wash again and cut into very small pieces.
4. Clean, wash and divide the spring onions into rings. Mix tomatoes, spring onions, chili peppers and a little paprika tomato paste as well as olive oil and rice syrup and season with sea salt and pepper.
5. Shape the lentil mixture into small rolls or balls. Set the oil in a pan and fry it brown all over or prepare it on the grill.
6. Arrange on plates and serve with the tomato salsa.

Nutrition:
Calories: 394
Protein: 20.1 g
Fat: 2.13 g
Carbohydrates: 76.77 g

47. Clear soup with liver dumplings

Preparation Time: 10 minutes **Cooking Time:** 40 minutes **Servings:** 2

Ingredients:

For the dumplings:
- 75 g veal liver
- 1 red onion, small
- Parsley, to taste
- ½ tbsp. olive oil

For the soup:
- 1 organic carrot
- 50 g of celery
- 2 spring onions
- 35 g breadcrumbs
- 1 organic egg size M
- Sea salt and black pepper
- Nutmeg, grated, optional

- ½ tbsp. oil
- Bay leaf, optional
- 500 ml of vegetable stock

Directions:
1. Turn the liver through a meat grinder (or have it made by the butcher).
2. Peel and cut the onion. Wash, dry and chop parsley.

3. Set the oil in a saucepan, sauté the onion briefly, add the parsley and sauté briefly. Then let it cool down.
4. Place the liver with the breadcrumbs in a bowl, add the onion-parsley mixture and egg and knead, salt and pepper. If you like, add some nutmeg and knead. Shape the mixture into about 6 dumplings and place in the refrigerator.
5. Now wash and dry the vegetables for the soup thoroughly. Cut the carrot into slices, cut the celery into bite-sized pieces and finally cut the spring onion into rolls. Warmth a little oil in a saucepan, cook the carrot, celery and spring onion together with the bay leaf for about 5 minutes. Then season with sea salt and pepper. Add the vegetable stock and simmer the soup over medium heat (about 10 minutes).
6. Finally add the dumplings and simmer for another 10 minutes.
7. When the dumplings stay to afloat to the surface they are done.
8. Serve the soup with the liver dumplings.

Nutrition:
Calories: 217
Protein: 13.41 g
Fat: 13.63 g
Carbohydrates: 10.73 g

48. Beef steaks with green asparagus

Preparation Time: 15 minutes **Cooking Time:** 20 minutes **Servings:** 4

Ingredients:
- 500 g asparagus, green
- 40 g herb butter
- 2 beef fillet steaks (approx. 150 g each)
- 1 dried tomato pickled in oil
- 50 g ricotta
- Sea salt and black pepper
- Herbs, fresh e.g., B. oregano, basil
- 1 tbsp. oil for frying and capers, as desired (optional)
- Also: aluminum foil and toothpicks or small wooden skewers

Directions:
1. Wash the asparagus and skin the lower ends. Prepare two pieces of baking paper or aluminum foil and spread the asparagus on top. Put the herb butter on the asparagus, close the foil tightly, put on the grill for about 10 - 15 minutes.
2. Dab steaks with a little paper towel, cut a pocket. Drain the tomatoes and cut into small pieces. Put the ricotta and capers in a bowl, wash, dry and chop the herbs and add them as well.
3. Mix everything well and season with sea salt and pepper. Pour the finished cream into the steaks and seal the openings with a toothpick.
4. Finally, season the steaks with sea salt and pepper, brush with the oil and grill depending on the degree of cooking required (approx. 5-8 minutes on each side).
5. Arrange the steaks with the asparagus, add the rest of the cream and serve hot.

Nutrition:
Calories: 339
Protein: 18.91 g
Fat: 27.06 g
Carbohydrates: 6.31 g

49. Broccoli Omelet

Preparation Time: 5 minutes **Cooking Time:** 1.5-2 hours **Servings:** 2

Ingredients:
- 2 garlic cloves, minced
- 3 eggs
- ½ yellow onion, chopped
- ¼ cup milk
- ½ cup broccoli florets
- ¼ teaspoon black pepper
- ½ tomato, chopped
- ⅛ teaspoon chili powder
- ½ tablespoon Parmesan cheese, shredded
- ¾ cups Cheddar cheese, shredded
- ⅛ teaspoon salt
- ⅛ cup green onions, chopped
- ⅛ teaspoon garlic powder

Directions:
1. Spill the eggs, milk, and spices in a bowl.
2. To the egg mixture, add onions along with the garlic, parmesan cheese, and broccoli. Whisk well until combined, and then pour the egg mixture into a slow cooker.
3. Close the lid and cook for about 1 ½ hour to 2 hours on high.
4. Remove the cover when the cooking time is over and then sprinkle the shredded cheddar cheese on top. Close the lid again and then turn off the slow cooker.
5. Let rest for about 10 minutes, until the cheddar cheese has melted.
6. When done, cut the omelet into quarters and then serve.

7. Garnish the servings with chopped green onion and fresh tomato. Enjoy!

Nutrition:

Calories: 423

Fat: 28g

Carbohydrates: 13g

Protein: 29g

50. Apple Cinnamon Oatmeal

Preparation Time: 10 minutes **Cooking Time:** 8 hours **Servings:** 4

Ingredients:

- 2 peeled and sliced apples
- 1 tbsp. cinnamon

What you'll need from store cupboard:

- Pinch of salt
- ⅓ Cup brown sugar
- 2 cups rolled oats, old-fashioned
- 4 cups water

Directions:

1. Place the apples in the crockpot bottom then add cinnamon and sugar over the apples. Stir to mix.
2. Add the oats over apples evenly then add salt and water. Do not stir.
3. Cover and cook for about 8-9 hours on low or cook overnight.
4. Stir well; making sure oats are not at the bottom.
5. Serve.

Nutrition:

Calories: 232.4

Fat: 3.1g

Carbohydrates: 53g

Protein: 5.2g

Sugars: 20.9g

Fiber: 6g

Sodium: 4.9mg

51. Nutty Steel-cut Oatmeal with Blueberries

Preparation Time: 5 minutes **Cooking Time:** 30 minutes **Servings:** 2

Ingredients:

- 1 ½ cups water
- ½ cup steel-cut oats
- 1 ½ tablespoons almond butter
- ½ teaspoon ground cinnamon
- ¼ teaspoon ground nutmeg
- Pinch ground ginger
- ½ cup blueberries
- ¼ cup whole almonds

Directions:

1. Over high-heat, put the water in a medium saucepan, and bring the liquid to a boil.
2. Spill in the oats and reduce the heat to low so they simmer gently.
3. Simmer the oats uncovered for about 20 minutes, until they are tender.
4. Stir in the almond butter, cinnamon, nutmeg, and ginger, and simmer for an additional 10 minutes.
5. Serve topped with blueberries and whole almonds.

Nutrition:

Calories: 246

Carbohydrates: 24g

Fiber: 5g

Protein: 8g

Sodium: 2mg

Fat: 14g

52. Slow "Roasted" Tomatoes

Preparation Time: 5 minutes **Cooking Time:** 1 hour 15 minutes **Servings:** 2

Ingredients:

- ½ tablespoon balsamic vinegar
- 1 large firm under-ripe tomato, halved crosswise
- 1 garlic clove, minced
- 1 teaspoon olive oil
- ½ teaspoon dried basil, crushed
- ½ cup breadcrumbs, coarse, soft whole-wheat
- Dried rosemary, crushed
- 1 tablespoon Parmesan cheese, grated
- Salt
- ¼ teaspoon dried oregano, crushed
- Chopped fresh basil, optional

Directions:

1. Using cooking spray, coat the unheated slow cooker lightly. Then add tomatoes to the bottom of the slow cooker, cut side up.
2. In a bowl, combine vinegar together with garlic, oil, rosemary, dried basil, and salt, and then spoon the mixture over the tomatoes in the slow cooker evenly.

3. Close the lid and cook for either 2 hours on low, or 1 hour on high.
4. Over medium preheat a skillet, and then add the breadcrumbs. Cook as you stir constantly until lightly browned, for about 2-3 minutes. Remove from heat when done and then stir in the parmesan.
5. When through, remove tomatoes from the slow cooker and put them on the serving plates, and then drizzle over tomatoes with the cooking liquid. Then sprinkle with the breadcrumb mixture and let rest for 10 minutes to absorb the flavors.
6. Garnish with basil if need be and then serve. Enjoy!

Nutrition:
Calories: 96
Fat: 4g
Carbohydrates: 13g
Protein: 3g

53. Tomato-Herb Omelet

Preparation Time: 10 minutes **Cooking Time:** 10 minutes **Servings:** 2

Ingredients:
- 1 tablespoon coconut oil, divided
- 2 scallions, green and white parts, chopped
- 1 teaspoon minced garlic
- 2 tomatoes, chopped, liquid squeezed out
- 6 eggs, beaten
- ½ teaspoon chopped fresh thyme
- ½ teaspoon chopped fresh basil
- ½ teaspoon chopped fresh chives
- ½ teaspoon chopped fresh oregano
- ⅛ teaspoon sea salt
- Pinch ground nutmeg
- Pinch freshly ground black pepper
- Chopped fresh parsley, for garnish

Directions:
1. Put a small saucepan over medium heat before adding 1 teaspoon of coconut oil.
2. Sauté the scallions and garlic for about 3 minutes, until the vegetables are softened.
3. Add the tomatoes and sauté for 3 minutes. Remove the saucepan from the heat and set aside.
4. Spill together the eggs, thyme, basil, chives, oregano, salt, nutmeg, and pepper in a medium bowl.
5. Put a large skillet over medium-high heat before adding the remaining 2 teaspoons of oil. Swirl the oil until it coats the skillet.
6. Spill in the egg mixture, and swirl until the eggs start to firm up-do not stir the eggs. Lift the edges of the firmed eggs to let the uncooked egg flow at the bottom.
7. When the eggs are almost done, spoon the tomato mixture onto one-half of the eggs.
8. Fold the uncovered side over the tomato mixture and cook for a minute longer.
9. Cut the omelet in half, sprinkle with parsley, and serve.

Nutrition:
Calories: 306
Carbohydrates: 13g
Fiber: 6g
Protein: 19g
Sodium: 312mg
Fat: 21g

54. Mouth-Watering Egg Casserole

Preparation Time: 15 minutes **Cooking Time:** 10 hours **Servings:** 2

Ingredients:
- 10oz ham, ½-inch slices
- ½ cup thinly sliced button mushrooms
- 1 tbsp. seeded red capsicum, thinly sliced

What you'll need from store cupboard:
- ¼ cup diced potatoes, cooked
- 1 tbsp. drained tomatoes, sun-dried and chopped up
- ¼ cup thawed and drained spinach, chopped and frozen
- 10oz diced Swiss cheese
- 10oz goat feta cheese
- ¼ cup thawed artichoke hearts, frozen and quartered
- Whole basil leaves, fresh
- 2 eggs
- 1 cup whole milk
- 1 tbsp. Dijon mustard
- Sea salt to taste
- Black pepper freshly cracked to taste

Directions:
1. Place a coated crockpot liner with cooking oil inside a crockpot, 2-qt
2. Grill the ham pieces for about 4 minutes until crisp. Retain the fat.
3. Sauté mushrooms and capsicum in the fat and butter for about 4 minutes until soft.
4. Place potatoes in the crockpot base and on top, then place an even layer of mushroom-capsicum mixture

5. Add half of artichokes, tomatoes, and spinach in layers then sprinkle with half Swiss cheese, followed by remaining vegetables, then remaining cheese and feta cheese.
6. Meanwhile, combine eggs, milk, and mustard in a bowl then pour over to settle through on the dish.
7. Place ham on top.
8. Seal and cook for about 8 hours on low then use the liner to remove the casserole.
9. Rest for about 10 minutes, then detach the liner.
10. Slice the casserole and garnish with basil leaves.
11. Serve alongside with green salad, leafy.

Nutrition:

Calories: 297
Fat: 17g
Carbohydrates: 20.8g
Protein: 15.8g,
Sugars: 10.2g
Fiber: 2.4g
Sodium: 416mg
Potassium: 617mg

55. Amazing Overnight Apple and Cinnamon Oatmeal

Preparation Time: 10 minutes **Cooking Time:** 7 hours **Servings:** 2

Ingredients:

- ¾ cup coconut milk
- 1 diced whole apple

What you'll need from store cupboard:

- 1 tbsp. coconut oil
- ¾ cup water, fresh

- ½ cup steel cut oats
- ½ tbsp. raw honey

- ¼ tbsp. salt to taste, sea
- 1 tbsp. cinnamon

Directions:

1. Spray your crockpot with cooking oil. This is to prevent food from sticking.
2. Add water, coconut milk, apples, oats, coconut oil, raw honey, salt, and cinnamon. Stir to combine.
3. Cover and cook for about 6-7 hours on low.
4. Serve hot with favorite toppings.

Nutrition:

Calories: 284
Fat: 17.9g
Carbohydrates: 30.3g
Protein: 4.2g
Sugars: 1.3g
Fiber: 4.7g
Sodium: 30mg
Potassium: 90mg

56. Zoodles with Pea Pesto

Preparation Time: 10 minutes **Cooking Time:** 10 minutes **Servings:** 2

Ingredients:

- 1 ½ zucchini
- 1 tablespoon extra-virgin olive oil

- Pinch sea salt
- Pea Pesto

Directions:

1. Cut the zucchini lengthwise into long strips using a vegetable peeler. Use a knife to cut the strips into the desired width. Alternatively, use a spiralizer to cut the zucchini into noodles.
2. In a large skillet, the olive oil is heated until it shimmers over medium-high heat. Add the zucchini and cook until softened for about 3 minutes. Add the sea salt.
3. Toss the zucchini noodles with the pesto.

Nutrition:

Calories: 348
Fat: 30g
Sodium: 343mg
Carbohydrates: 13g
Fiber: 1g
Protein: 10g

57. Shrimp Peri-Peri

Preparation Time: 10 minutes **Cooking Time:** 15 minutes **Servings:** 2

Ingredients:

- Peri-Peri Sauce
- ½ lb. large shrimp

- 1 tablespoon extra-virgin olive oil
- Sea salt

Directions:

1. Preheat the oven broiler on high.
2. In a small pot, bring the Peri-Peri Sauce to a simmer.
3. Meanwhile, place the cleaned shrimp on a rimmed baking sheet, deveined-side down. Garnish with olive oil and sprinkle with salt.
4. Broil until opaque, about 5 minutes. Serve with the sauce on the side for dipping or spooned over the top of the shrimp.

Nutrition:

Calories: 279　　　Sodium: 464mg　　　Fiber: 3g
Fat: 16g　　　Carbohydrates: 10g　　　Protein: 24g

58. Halibut with Lime and Cilantro

Preparation Time: 30 minutes　　**Cooking Time:** 45 minutes　　**Servings:** 2

Ingredients:
- 2 tbsp. lime juice
- 1 tbsp. chopped fresh cilantro
- 1 tsp. olive or canola oil
- 1 clove garlic, finely chopped
- 2 halibut or salmon steaks
- Freshly ground pepper
- ½ cup chunky-style salsa

Directions:
1. In a shallow glass or in a resalable food-storage plastic bag, merge lime juice, cilantro, oil, and garlic. Attach halibut, turning several times to coat with marinade. Seal; refrigerate 15 minutes, turning once.
2. Heat gas or charcoal grill. Remove halibut from marinade, discard marinade.
3. Place halibut on the grill over medium heat. Cover grill: cook 10 to 20 minutes, turning once, until halibut flakes easily with a fork. Sprinkle it with pepper. Serve with salsa.

Nutrition:
Calories: 190　　　Sodium: 600mg　　　Sugars: 2g
Fat: 4.5g　　　Carbohydrates: 6g　　　Protein: 32g
Cholesterol: 90mg　　　Fiber: 0g

59. Autumn Pork Chop with Red Cabbage and Apples

Preparation Time: 15 minutes　　**Cooking Time:** 30 minutes　　**Servings:** 2

Ingredients:
- ⅛ Cup apple cider vinegar
- 1 tablespoon granulated sweetener
- 2 (4 oz.) pork chops, about 1 inch thick
- ½ tablespoon extra-virgin olive oil
- ¼ red cabbage, finely shredded
- ½ sweet onion, thinly sliced
- ½ apple, peeled, cored, and sliced
- ½ teaspoon chopped fresh thyme

Directions:
1. Scourge together the vinegar and sweetener. Set it aside.
2. Season the pork with salt and pepper.
3. Position a big skillet over medium-high heat and add the olive oil.
4. Cook the pork chops until no longer pink, turning once, about 8 minutes per side.
5. Put chops aside.
6. Attach the cabbage and onion to the skillet and saute until the vegetables have softened about 5 minutes.
7. Add the vinegar mixture and the apple slices to the skillet and bring the mixture to boiling point.
8. Adjust low-heat and simmer for 5 additional minutes.
9. Return the pork chops to the skillet, along with any accumulated juices and thyme, cover, and cook for more minutes.

Nutrition:
Calories: 306　　　Fiber: 6g　　　Sodium: 312mg
Carbohydrates: 13g　　　Protein: 19g　　　Fat: 21g

60. Orange-Marinated Pork Tenderloin

Preparation Time: 2 hours　　**Cooking Time:** 30 minutes　　**Servings:** 2

Ingredients:
- ⅛ Cup freshly squeezed orange juice
- 1 teaspoon orange zest
- 1 teaspoon minced garlic
- ½ teaspoon low-sodium soy sauce
- ½ teaspoon grated fresh ginger
- ½ teaspoon honey
- ¾ pounds pork tenderloin roast
- ½ tablespoon extra-virgin olive oil

Directions:
1. Blend together the orange juice, zest, garlic, soy sauce, ginger, and honey.
2. Pour the marinade into a resalable plastic bag and add the pork tenderloin.
3. Detach as much air as possible and seal the bag. Marinate the pork in the refrigerator, turning the bag a few times, for 2 hours.
4. Preheat the oven to 400F.

5. Pull out tenderloin from the marinade and discard the marinade.
6. Position a big ovenproof skillet over medium-high heat and add the oil.
7. Sear the pork tenderloin on all sides.
8. Position skillet to the oven and roast for 25 minutes.
9. Put aside for 10 minutes before serving.

Nutrition:
Calories: 217
Protein: 13.41 g
Fat: 13.63 g
Carbohydrates: 10.73 g

Meat

61. Pork Medallions with Cherry Sauce

Preparation Time: 25 minutes **Cooking Time:** 6 to 8 minutes **Servings:** 4

Ingredients:
- 1 pork tenderloin (1 to 1¼ lb.), cut into ½-inch slices
- ½ teaspoon garlic-pepper blend
- 2 teaspoons olive oil
- ¾ cup cherry preserves
- 2 tablespoons chopped shallots
- 1 tablespoon Dijon mustard
- 1 tablespoon balsamic vinegar
- 1 clove garlic, finely chopped

Directions:
1. Drizzle both sides of pork with garlic-pepper blend.
2. In 12-inch skillet, heat 1 tsp. of the oil over medium-high heat. Attach pork; cook 6 to 8 minutes, turning once, until pork is browned and meat thermometer inserted in center reads 145F. Remove pork from skillet; keep warm.
3. In same skillet, mix remaining teaspoon oil, the preserves, shallots, mustard, vinegar and garlic, scraping any brown bits from bottom of skillet. Heat to boiling. Lower heat: simmer uncovered 1 minutes or until reduced to about ½ cup. Serve sauce over pork slices.

Nutrition:
Calories: 330
Fat: 7g
Protein: 23g
Carbohydrates: 44g
Sugars: 30g
Fiber: 1g
Sodium: 170mg

62. Pork Chops Pomodoro

Preparation Time: 0 minutes **Cooking Time:** 30 minutes **Servings:** 6

Ingredients:
- 2 pounds boneless pork loin chops
- ¾ teaspoon sea salt
- ½ tsp. freshly ground black pepper
- 2 tbsp. extra-virgin olive oil

- 2 garlic cloves, hashed
- ½ cup of vegetable broth or chicken broth
- ½ tsp. Italian seasoning
- 1 tbsp. capers, drained
- 2 cups cherry tomatoes
- 2 tbsp. fresh basil or flat-leaf parsley
- Spiralized zucchini noodles
- Lemon wedges for serving

Directions:
1. Set the pork chops dry with paper towels, then flavor them all over with the salt and pepper.
2. Set the Instant Pot and heat 1 tablespoon of the oil for 2 minutes. Set the oil to coat the bottom of the pot. Using tongs, attach half of the pork chops in a single layer and set for about 3 minutes. Set the chops to a plate. Redo with the remaining 1 tbsp. oil and pork chops.
3. Attach the garlic to the pot and sauté for about 1 minute. Spill in the broth, Italian seasoning, and capers. Transfer the pork chops to the pot. Attach the tomatoes in an even layer on top of the chops.
4. Seal the lid and set the Pressure Release to Sealing. Push the Cancel button to reset the cooking program, then select the Pressure Cook at high pressure.
5. Set the tomatoes and some of the cooking liquid on top of the pork chops. Drizzle with the basil and serve right away, with zucchini noodles and lemon wedges on the side.

Nutrition:
Calories: 265
Fat: 13g
Protein: 31g
Carbohydrates: 3g
Sugars: 2g
Fiber: 1g
Sodium: 460mg

63. Meatballs Barley Soup

Preparation Time: 15 minutes **Cooking Time:** 35 minutes **Servings:** 6

Ingredients:
- 2 cups of water
- 1 can of Great Northern beans, washed and drained,
- ½ cup of quick-cooking barley
- 4 cups of fresh baby spinach leaves,
- 1 pound 90% or higher lean ground beef
- 1 tablespoon of olive oil
- 3 medium carrots, peeled and coarsely chopped
- 2 medium yellow and/or red bell peppers, seeded and cut into bite-size strips
- 1 medium onion, chopped
- 2 cups of less-sodium beef stock
- ¾ cup of soft whole-wheat breadcrumbs
- ¼ cup of refrigerated or frozen egg product, thawed, or 1 egg, lightly beaten
- 4 cloves garlic, minced, divided
- 2 tsp. of chopped fresh rosemary, or ½ tsp. of crushed dried rosemary, divided
- ¼ teaspoon of ground pepper

Directions:
1. Preheat oven to 350 F.
2. Combine breadcrumbs, egg, half of the garlic, half of the rosemary, and the ground pepper in a large bowl.
3. Add ground beef; mix well. Shape the meat mixture into a 1 ½-inch meatball.
4. Place the meatballs in a foil-lined 15x10-inch baking pan.
5. Bake for about 15 minutes. Set aside.
6. Warmth oil over medium heat in a large pot. Add carrot, bell pepper, onion, and the remaining garlic; cook for 5 minutes, stirring occasionally.
7. Add beef stock, water, Great Northern beans, barley, and the remaining rosemary.
8. Bring to boiling; reduce heat. Seal and simmer for about 15 minutes or until the barley is tender.
9. Add the meatballs to the barley mixture, heat through. Stir in spinach just before serving.

Nutrition:
Calories: 325
Fat: 8g
Protein: 35g
Carbohydrates: 26g
Sugars: 6g
Fiber: 4g
Sodium: 560mg

64. Beef Massaman Curry

Preparation Time: 10 minutes **Cooking Time:** 2 hours **Servings:** 4

Ingredients:
- 2 onions, roughly chopped
- 4 kaffir lime leaves
- 1.5 tablespoon of tamarind paste
- 1.5 tablespoon of fish sauce
- 75grams of unsalted peanuts
- 400ml of coconut milk
- 3 tablespoons of massaman curry paste
- 550grams of stewing beef steak, diced

- 300grams of potatoes, diced

Directions:
1. Preheat the oven to 200C.
2. Roast the peanuts for 4-5 minutes.
3. Once they have cooled, chop them roughly.
4. Then lower the oven temperature to 200C.
5. Heat 2 tbsp. of coconut cream in a casserole dish that has a lid.
6. Merge in the curry paste and fry for a minute.
7. Set in the beef and cook for about 6 minutes.
8. Attach the remaining coconut cream with half a can of water, the potatoes, onions, fish sauce, kaffir leaves, tamarind paste, and most of the peanuts.
9. Place the lid on the curry. Set in the oven for 2 hours until tender.
10. Sprinkle the sliced chili and the rest of the peanuts.
11. Serve and enjoy!

- 1 red chili, seeds detached and finely sliced, to serve

Nutrition:
Calories: 320 Carbohydrates: 48g Sodium: 420mg
Fat: 4g Sugar: 1.1g
Protein: 23g Fiber: 3g

65. Old Fashioned Beef Soup with Vegetables

Preparation Time: 25 minutes **Cooking Time:** 4 hours 15 minutes **Servings:** 10

Ingredients:
- 1 bay leaf
- ¼ teaspoon of dried marjoram
- ¼ teaspoon of dried oregano
- 2 pounds of beef soup bones
- 1 large carrot, skinned and cut into large chunks
- 1 small green bell pepper, chopped
- 2 tablespoons of butter
- 1 onion, coarsely chopped
- 4 stalks celery, chopped
- ⅓ pound of lean round steak, cut into ½-inch cubes
- 1-quart of beef stock
- 1-quart of water
- ¼ cup of dry black beans
- ¼ cup of dried split peas
- ¼ cup of brown rice
- 1 large potato, skinned and cut into large chunks
- ¼ cup of elbow macaroni
- 1 cup of crushed tomatoes in puree
- ¼ cup of chopped cabbage
- 1 cup of red wine
- salt and ground black pepper to taste

Directions:
1. In a large stockpot, dissolve the butter over medium heat; cook the onion, steak, and celery in the melted butter for about 7 to 10 minutes until the onions caramelize.
2. Add the beef, stock, bay leaf, water, oregano, marjoram, and soup bones; lower the heat to medium-low and simmer for about 3 hours.
3. Add the carrot, potato, bell pepper, black beans, rice, split peas, tomatoes in puree, macaroni, red wine, and cabbage to the stockpot.
4. Simmer for about an hour.
5. Remove the soup bones, scraping any meat from them back into the pot.
6. Season with pepper and salt to serve.

Nutrition:
Calories: 140 Carbohydrates: 3g Sodium: 141mg
Fat: 7g Sugars: 1g
Protein: 18g Fiber: 1g

66. Beef and Red Bean Chili

Preparation Time: 10 minutes **Cooking Time:** 6 hours **Servings:** 4

Ingredients:
- 1 cup dry red beans
- 1 tablespoon olive oil
- 2 pounds boneless beef chuck
- 1 large onion, coarsely chopped
- 1 (14 ounce) can beef broth
- 2 chipotle chili peppers in adobo sauce
- 2 teaspoons dried oregano, crushed
- 1 teaspoon ground cumin
- ½ teaspoon salt
- 1 (14.5 ounce) can tomatoes with mild green chilis
- 1 (15 ounce) can tomato sauce
- ¼ cup snipped fresh cilantro
- 1 medium red sweet pepper

Directions:
1. Rinse out the beans and place them into a Dutch oven or big saucepan, then add in water enough to cover them. Allow the beans to boil then drop the heat down. Simmer the beans without a cover for 10 minutes. Take off the heat and keep covered for an hour.
2. In a big fry pan, heat up the oil upon medium-high heat, then cook onion and half the beef until they brown a bit over medium-high heat. Move into a 3 ½- or 4-quart crockery cooker.
3. Do this again with what's left of the beef. Add in tomato sauce, tomatoes (not drained), salt, cumin, oregano, adobo sauce, chipotle peppers, and broth, stirring to blend. Strain out and rinse beans and stir in the cooker.
4. Cook while sealed on a low setting for around 10-12 hours or on high setting for 5-6 hours. Spoon the chili into bowls or mugs and top with sweet pepper and cilantro.

Nutrition:
Calories: 303
Fat: 7g
Protein: 32g
Carbohydrates: 27g
Sugars: 7g
Fiber: 4g
Sodium: 310mg

67. Cider Pork Stew

Preparation Time: 9 minutes **Cooking Time:** 12 hours **Servings:** 3

Ingredients:
- 2 pounds pork shoulder roast
- 3 medium cubed potatoes
- 3 medium carrots
- 2 medium onions, sliced
- 1 cup coarsely chopped apple
- ½ cup coarsely chopped celery
- 3 tablespoons quick-cooking tapioca
- 2 cups apple juice
- 1 teaspoon salt
- 1 teaspoon caraway seeds
- ¼ teaspoon black pepper

Directions:
1. Chop the meat into 1-in. cubes. In the 3.5- 5.5 qt. slow cooker, mix the tapioca, celery, apple, onions, carrots, potatoes and meat. Whisk in pepper, caraway seeds, salt and apple juice.
2. Keep covered and cook over low heat setting for 10-12 hours. If you want, use the celery leaves to decorate each of the servings.

Nutrition:
Calories: 268
Fat: 10g
Protein: 25g
Carbohydrates: 26g
Sugars: 7g
Fiber: 7g
Sodium: 3887mg

68. Cuban Pulled Pork Sandwich

Preparation Time: 6 minutes **Cooking Time:** 5 hours **Servings:** 5

Ingredients:
- 1 teaspoon dried oregano, crushed
- ¾ teaspoon ground cumin
- ½ teaspoon ground coriander
- ¼ teaspoon salt
- ¼ teaspoon black pepper
- ¼ teaspoon ground allspice
- 1 2 to 2½-pound boneless pork shoulder roast
- 1 tablespoon olive oil
- Nonstick cooking spray
- 2 cups sliced onions
- 2 green sweet peppers, cut into bite-size strips
- ½ to 1 fresh jalapeño pepper
- 4 cloves garlic, minced
- ¼ cup orange juice
- ¼ cup lime juice
- 6 heart-healthy wheat hamburger buns, toasted
- 2 tablespoons jalapeño mustard

Directions:
1. Mix allspice, oregano, black pepper, cumin, salt, and coriander together in a small bowl. Press each side of the roast into the spice mixture. On medium-high heat, heat oil in a big non-stick pan; put in roast. Cook for 5mins until both sides of the roast is light brown, turn the roast one time.
2. Using a cooking spray, grease a 3 ½ or 4qt slow cooker; arrange the garlic, onions, jalapeno, and green peppers in a layer. Pour in lime juice and orange juice. Slice the roast if needed to fit inside the cooker; put on top of the vegetables covered or 4 ½-5hrs on high heat setting.

3. Move roast to a cutting board using a slotted spoon. Drain the cooking liquid and keep the jalapeno, green peppers, and onions. Shred the roast with 2 forks then place it back in the cooker. Remove fat from the liquid. Mix half cup of cooking liquid and reserved vegetables into the cooker. Pour in more cooking liquid if desired. Discard the remaining cooking liquid.
4. Slather mustard on rolls. Split the meat between the bottom roll halves. Add avocado on top if desired. Place the roll tops to sandwiches.

Nutrition:
Calories: 321
Fat: 13g
Protein: 11g
Carbohydrates: 42g
Sugars: 7g
Fiber: 11g
Sodium: 412mg

69. Sunday Pot Roast

Preparation Time: 10 minutes **Cooking Time:** 1 hour 45 minutes **Servings:** 10

Ingredients:
- 1 (3- to 4-pound / 1.4- to 1.8-kg) beef rump roast
- 2 teaspoons kosher salt, divided
- 2 tablespoons avocado oil
- 1 large onion, coarsely hashed (about 1½ cups)
- 4 large carrots, each divide into 4 pieces
- 1 tablespoon minced garlic
- 3 cups low-sodium beef broth
- 1 teaspoon freshly ground black pepper
- 1 tablespoon dried parsley
- 2 tablespoons all-purpose flour

Directions:
1. Rub the roast all over with 1 teaspoon of the salt.
2. Warmth the pot and pour in the avocado oil.
3. Carefully set the roast in the pot and sear it for 6 to 9 minutes on each side.
4. Set the roast from the pot to a plate.
5. In order, place the onion, carrots, and garlic in the pot. Form the roast on top of the vegetables along with any juices that accumulated on the plate.
6. In a bowl, whisk together the broth, remaining 1 teaspoon of salt, pepper, and parsley. Pour the broth mixture over the roast.
7. Seal and lock the pressure cooker. Set the valve to sealing.
8. Set on high pressure for 1 hr. and 30 minutes. When the cooking is complete, hit Cancel and allow the pressure to release naturally.
9. Once the pin drops, unseal and remove the lid.
10. Using large slotted spoons, bring the roast and vegetables to a serving platter while you make the gravy.
11. Using a large spoon or fat separator, detach the fat from the juices. Choose the electric pressure cooker to the Sauté setting and set the liquid to a boil.
12. In a small bowl, spill together the flour and 4 tbsp. of water to make a slurry. Spill the slurry into the pot, whisking occasionally, until the gravy is the thickness you like. Season with salt and pepper, if necessary.
13. Serve with the gravy.

Nutrition:
Calories: 245
Fat: 10g
Protein: 33g
Carbohydrates: 6g
Sugars: 2g
Fiber: 1g
Sodium: 397mg

70. Broccoli Beef Stir-Fry

Preparation Time: 10 minutes **Cooking Time:** 15 minutes **Servings:** 4

Ingredients:
- 2 tablespoons extra-virgin olive oil
- 1 pound (454 g) sirloin steak, cut into ¼-inch-thick strips
- 2 cups broccoli florets
- 1 garlic clove, minced
- 1 teaspoon peeled and grated fresh ginger
- 2 tablespoons reduced-sodium soy sauce
- ¼ cup beef broth
- ½ teaspoon Chinese hot mustard
- Pinch red pepper flakes

Directions:
1. In a skillet over medium-high heat, warmth the olive oil until it shimmers. Add the beef. Cook, stirring, until it browns, 3 to 5 minutes. With a slotted spoon, detach the beef from the oil and set it aside on a plate.
2. Add the broccoli to the oil. Cook, stirring, until it is crisp-tender, about 4 minutes.
3. Add the garlic and ginger and cook, stirring constantly, for 30 seconds.
4. Set the beef to the pan, along with any juices that have collected.
5. In a small bowl, whisk together the soy sauce, broth, mustard, and red pepper flakes.

6. Attach the soy sauce mixture to the skillet and cook, stirring, until everything warms through, about 3 minutes.

Nutrition:

Calories: 227

Fat: 11g

Protein: 27g

Carbohydrates: 5g

Sugars: 0g

Fiber: 1g

Sodium: 375mg

71. Beef and Pepper Fajita Bowls

Preparation Time: 10 minutes **Cooking Time:** 15 minutes **Servings:** 4

Ingredients:

- 4 tablespoons extra-virgin olive oil, divided
- 1 head cauliflower, riced
- 1 pound (454 g) sirloin steak, cut into ¼-inch-thick strips
- 1 red bell pepper, seeded and sliced
- 1 onion, thinly sliced
- 2 garlic cloves, minced
- Juice of 2 limes
- 1 teaspoon chili powder

Directions:

1. In a skillet over medium-high heat, warmth 2 tablespoons of olive oil until it shimmers. Attach the cauliflower. Cook and stir.
2. Clean out the skillet. Attach the remaining 2 tablespoons of oil to the skillet and heat it on medium-high until it shimmers. Attach the steak and cook until it browns. Use a slotted spoon to detach the steak from the oil in the pan and set aside.
3. Attach the bell pepper and onion to the pan. Cook and stir until they start to brown, about 5 minutes.
4. Attach d the garlic and cook, stirring constantly, for 30 seconds.
5. Set the beef along with any juices that have collected and the cauliflower to the pan. Attach the lime juice and chili powder. Cook and stir until everything is warmed through, 2 to 3 minutes.

Nutrition:

Calories: 310

Fat: 18g

Protein: 27g

Carbohydrates: 13g

Sugars: 2g

Fiber: 3g

Sodium: 93mg

72. Meat skewers with polenta

Preparation Time: 10 minutes **Cooking Time:** 15 minutes **Servings:** 4

Ingredients:

- 130 g polenta, instant
- Vegetable broth
- 1 organic lemon
- 2 tbsp. parmesan, grated
- Chili flakes, to taste
- 250 g of green asparagus
- 2 carrots, large
- 1 ½ tbsp. oil for frying
- Sea salt and black pepper, fresh
- 4 tbsp. sour cream
- 250 g pork schnitzel
- Paprika powder, noble sweet and parsley, fresh
- Metal skewers

Directions:

1. Prepare the polenta with stock according to the instructions on the packet. Wash the lemon, make zest and squeeze. Season the polenta with 2 teaspoons of lemon juice, a little zest, cheese and chili to taste.
2. Wash and clean the asparagus and carrots, cut lengthways into thin strips with a peeler.
3. Dab the schnitzel with kitchen paper and pound, cut into strips, then slide on skewers in waves, season with sea salt and pepper. Wash, dry and chop parsley.
4. Warmth a pan with oil and fry the skewers for about 5 minutes (the meat should be done).
5. Keep the skewers warm in the oven. Fry the vegetables in oil until al dente, then season with salt and pepper. Pour in a little broth, bring to the boil. And finally stir in the sour cream.
6. Arrange the skewers and vegetables on two plates and sprinkle with the parsley.

Nutrition:

Calories: 200

Fat: 8g

Protein: 30g

Carbohydrates: 1g

Sugars: 1g

Fiber: 0g

Sodium: 394mg

73. Chipotle Chili Pork Chops

Preparation Time: 5 minutes **Cooking Time:** 20 minutes **Servings:** 4

Ingredients:
- Juice and zest of 1 lime
- 1 tablespoon extra-virgin olive oil
- 1 tablespoon chipotle chili powder
- 2 teaspoons minced garlic
- 1 teaspoon ground cinnamon
- Pinch sea salt
- 4 (5-ounce / 142-g) pork chops, about 1 inch thick
- Lime wedges, for garnish

Directions:
1. Combine the lime juice and zest, oil, chipotle chili powder, garlic, cinnamon, and salt in a resalable plastic bag. Add the pork chops. Detach as much air as possible and seal the bag.
2. Marinate the chops in the refrigerator for at least 4 hours, and up to 24 hours, turning them several times.
3. Warmth the oven to 400F (205C) and set a rack on a baking sheet. Let the chops rest, then arrange them on the rack and discard the remaining marinade.
4. Roast the chops until cooked through, turning once about 10 minutes per side.
5. Serve with lime wedges.

Nutrition:
Calories: 204 Carbohydrates: 1g Sodium: 317mg
Fat: 9g Sugars: 1g
Protein: 30g Fiber: 0g

74. Lime-Parsley Lamb Cutlets

Preparation Time: 10 minutes **Cooking Time:** 10 minutes **Servings:** 4

Ingredients:
- ¼ cup extra-virgin olive oil
- ¼ cup freshly squeezed lime juice
- 2 tablespoons lime zest
- 2 tablespoons chopped fresh parsley
- Pinch sea salt
- Pinch freshly ground black pepper
- 12 lamb cutlets (about 1½ pounds / 680 g total)

Directions:
1. In a medium bowl, merge together the oil, lime juice, zest, parsley, salt, and pepper.
2. Transfer the marinade to a resalable plastic bag.
3. Attach the cutlets to the bag and remove as much air as possible before sealing.
4. Marinate the lamb for about 4 hours, turning the bag several times.
5. Preheat the oven to broil.
6. Detach the chops from the bag and arrange them on an aluminum foil-lined baking sheet. Discard the marinade.
7. Simmer the chops for 4 minutes per side for medium doneness.
8. Let the chops rest before serving.

Nutrition:
Calories: 413 Carbohydrates: 1g Sodium: 100mg
Fat: 29g Sugars: 0g
Protein: 31g Fiber: 0g

75. Traditional Beef Stroganoff

Preparation Time: 10 minutes **Cooking Time:** 30 minutes **Servings:** 4

Ingredients:
- 1 teaspoon extra-virgin olive oil
- 1 pound (454 g) top sirloin, cut into thin strips
- 1 cup sliced button mushrooms
- ½ sweet onion, finely chopped
- 1 teaspoon minced garlic
- 1 tablespoon whole-wheat flour
- ½ cup low-sodium beef broth
- ¼ cup dry sherry
- ½ cup fat-free sour cream
- 1 tablespoon chopped fresh parsley
- Sea salt and freshly ground black pepper

Directions:
1. Set a large skillet with medium-high heat and add the oil.
2. Sauté the beef until browned, about 10 minutes, then remove the beef with a slotted spoon to a plate and set it aside.

3. Attach the mushrooms, onion, and garlic to the skillet and sauté until lightly browned, about 5 minutes.
4. Whisk in the flour and then whisk in the beef broth and sherry.
5. Return the sirloin to the skillet and bring the mixture to a boil.
6. Set the heat to low and simmer until the beef is tender, about 10 minutes.
7. Stir in the sour cream and parsley. Season with salt and pepper.

Nutrition:
Calories: 257
Fat: 14g
Protein: 26g
Carbohydrates: 6g
Sugars: 1g
Fiber: 1g
Sodium: 141mg

76. Smothered Sirloin

Preparation Time: 15 minutes **Cooking Time:** 30 minutes **Servings:** 5

Ingredients:
- 1 pound (454 g) beef round sirloin tip
- 1 teaspoon freshly ground black pepper
- 1 teaspoon celery seeds
- 2 tablespoons extra-virgin olive oil
- 1 medium yellow onion, chopped
- ¼ cup chickpea flour
- 2 cups chicken broth, divided
- 2 celery stalks, thinly sliced
- 1 medium red bell pepper, chopped
- 2 garlic cloves, minced
- 2 tablespoons whole-wheat flour
- Generous pinch cayenne pepper
- Chopped fresh chives, for garnish (optional)
- Smoked paprika, for garnish (optional)

Directions:
1. In a bowl, season the steak on both sides with the black pepper and celery seeds.
2. Select the Sauté setting on an electric pressure cooker and combine the olive oil and onions. Cook and stir until the onions are ready but not burned.
3. Slowly add the chickpea flour, 1 tablespoon at a time, while stirring.
4. Add 1 cup of broth, ¼ cup at a time, as needed.
5. Stir in the celery, bell pepper, and garlic and cook for 3 to 5 minutes, or until softened.
6. Lay the beef on top of vegetables and pour the remaining 1 cup of broth on top.
7. Seal the lid and cook for 20 minutes.
8. Once cooking is complete, quick-release the pressure. Carefully remove the lid.
9. Remove the steak and vegetables from the pressure cooker, reserving the leftover liquid for the gravy base.
10. To make the gravy, add the whole-wheat flour and cayenne to the liquid in the pressure cooker, mixing continuously until thickened.
11. To serve, spoon the gravy over the steak and garnish with the chives (if using) and paprika (if using).

Nutrition:
Calories: 253
Fat: 13g
Protein: 22g
Carbohydrates: 10g
Sugars: 3g
Fiber: 2g
Sodium: 86mg

77. Loaded Cottage Pie

Preparation Time: 15 minutes **Cooking Time:** 60 minutes **Servings:** 6-8

Ingredients:
- 4 large russet potatoes, peeled and halved
- 3 tablespoons extra-virgin olive oil, divided
- 1 small onion, chopped
- 1 bunch collard greens, stemmed and thinly sliced
- 2 carrots, peeled and chopped
- 2 medium tomatoes, chopped
- 1 garlic clove, minced
- 1 pound (454 g) 90 percent lean ground beef
- ½ cup chicken broth
- 1 teaspoon Worcestershire sauce
- 1 teaspoon celery seeds
- 1 teaspoon smoked paprika
- ½ teaspoon dried chives
- ½ teaspoon ground mustard
- ½ teaspoon cayenne pepper

Directions:
1. Preheat the oven to 400F (205C).
2. Set a pot of water to a boil.
3. Attach the potatoes, and boil for 15 to 20 minutes, or until fork-tender.

4. Set the potatoes to a large bowl and mash with 1 tablespoon of olive oil.
5. In a large cast iron skillet, heat the remaining 2 tablespoons of olive oil.
6. Add the onion, collard greens, carrots, tomatoes, and garlic and sauté, stirring often, for 7 to 10 minutes until the vegetables are softened.
7. Add the beef, broth, Worcestershire sauce, celery seeds, and smoked paprika.
8. Spread the meat and vegetable mixture evenly onto the bottom of a casserole dish. Sprinkle the chives, ground mustard, and cayenne on top of the mixture. Drizzle the mashed potatoes evenly over the top.
9. Transfer the casserole dish to the oven, and bake for 30 minutes, or until the top is light golden brown.

Nutrition:
Calories: 440
Fat: 17g
Protein: 27g
Carbohydrates: 48g
Sugars: 6g
Fiber: 9g
Sodium: 107mg

78. Fresh Pot Pork Butt

Preparation Time: 10 minutes **Cooking Time:** 45 minutes **Servings:** 8

Ingredients:
- 2 tablespoons extra-virgin olive oil
- ¼ cup apple cider vinegar
- 1 tablespoon freshly ground black pepper
- 1 tablespoon dried oregano
- 1 small yellow onion, minced
- 2 scallions, white and green parts, minced
- 1 celery stalk, minced
- Juice of 1 lime
- 2 pounds (907 g) boneless pork butt
- 4 garlic cloves, sliced
- 1 cup chicken broth

Directions:
1. In a medium bowl, merge the oil, vinegar, pepper, oregano, onion, scallions, celery, and lime juice. Mix well until a paste is formed.
2. Score the pork with 1-inch-deep cuts in a diamond pattern on both sides. Push the garlic into the slits.
3. Massage the paste all over meat. Secure and refrigerate overnight or for at least 4 hours.
4. Select the Sauté setting on an electric pressure cooker. Cook the meat on each side.
5. Attach the broth, close and lock the lid, and set the pressure valve to sealing.
6. Change to the Manual setting and cook for 2 minutes.
7. Once cooking is complete, allow the pressure to release naturally. Carefully remove the lid.
8. Detach the pork from the pressure cooker and serve with Ranch Dressing.

Nutrition:
Calories: 287
Fat: 22g
Protein: 20g
Carbohydrates: 1g
Sugars: 1g
Fiber: 1g
Sodium: 88mg

79. Pork Diane

Preparation Time: 10 minutes **Cooking Time:** 20 minutes **Servings:** 4

Ingredients:
- 2 teaspoons Worcestershire sauce
- 1 tablespoon freshly squeezed lemon juice
- ¼ cup low-sodium chicken broth
- 2 teaspoons Dijon mustard
- 4 (5-ounce / 142-g) boneless pork top loin chops, about 1 inch thick
- Sea salt and freshly ground black pepper
- 1 teaspoon extra-virgin olive oil
- 2 teaspoons chopped fresh chives
- 1 teaspoon lemon zest

Directions:
1. Combine the Worcestershire sauce, lemon juice, broth, and Dijon mustard in a bowl. Stir to mix well.
2. On a clean work surface, massage the pork chops with salt and ground black pepper.
3. Heat the olive oil in a nonstick skillet over medium-high heat until shimmering.
4. Add the pork chops and sear for 16 minutes or until well browned. Flip the pork halfway through the cooking time. Transfer to a plate and set aside.
5. Pour the sauce mixture in the skillet and cook for minutes or until warmed through and lightly thickened. Mix in the chives and lemon zest.

6. Baste the pork with the sauce mixture and serve immediately.

Nutrition:
Calories: 355
Fat: 27.1g
Protein: 19.8g
Carbs: 5.9g
Fiber: 1.0g
Sugar: 4.0g
Sodium: 200mg

80. Autumn Pork Chops

Preparation Time: 15 minutes **Cooking Time:** 30 minutes **Servings:** 4

Ingredients:
- ¼ cup apple cider vinegar
- 2 tablespoons granulated sweetener
- 4 (4-ounce / 113-g) pork chops, about 1 inch thick
- Sea salt and freshly ground black pepper
- 1 tablespoon extra-virgin olive oil
- ½ red cabbage, finely shredded
- 1 sweet onion, thinly sliced
- 1 apple, peeled, cored, and sliced
- 1 teaspoon chopped fresh thyme

Directions:
1. In a small bowl, merge together the vinegar and sweetener. Set it aside.
2. Season the pork with salt and pepper.
3. Set a large skillet with medium-high heat and add the olive oil.
4. Cook the pork chops, turning once, about 8 minutes per side.
5. Bring the chops to a plate and set aside.
6. Attach the cabbage and onion to the skillet and sauté until the vegetables have softened, about 5 minutes.
7. Add the vinegar mixture and the apple slices to the skillet and bring the mixture to a boil.
8. Set the heat to low and simmer, covered, for 5 additional minutes.
9. Return the pork chops to the skillet, along with any accumulated juices and thyme, cover, and cook for 5 more minutes.

Nutrition:
Calories: 224
Fat: 8.1g
Protein: 26.1g
Carbohydrates: 12.1g
Fiber: 3.1g
Sugar: 8.0g
Sodium: 293mg

Poultry

81. Turkey Chili

Preparation Time: 15 minutes **Cooking Time:** 30 minutes **Servings:** 6

Ingredients:
- 1 tablespoon extra-virgin olive oil
- 1 pound lean ground turkey
- 1 large onion, diced
- 3 garlic cloves, minced
- 1 red bell pepper, seeded and diced
- 1 cup chopped celery
- 2 tablespoons chili powder
- 1 tablespoon ground cumin
- 1 (28-ounce) can reduced-salt diced tomatoes
- 1 can low-sodium kidney beans, drained and washed
- 2 cups low-sodium chicken broth
- ½ teaspoon salt
- Shredded cheddar cheese, for serving (optional)

Directions:
1. In a large pot, warmth the oil over medium heat. Attach the turkey, onion, and garlic, and cook, stirring regularly, until the turkey is cooked through.
2. Add the bell pepper, celery, chili powder, and cumin. Stir well and cook for 1 minute.
3. Add the tomatoes with their liquid, kidney beans, and chicken broth. Bring to a boil, set the heat to low and simmer for 20 minutes.
4. Season with the salt and serve topped with cheese (if using).

Nutrition:
Calories: 276
Fat: 10g
Protein: 23g
Carbohydrates: 27g
Sugars: 7g
Fiber: 8g
Sodium: 556mg

82. Barbecue Turkey Burger Sliders

Preparation Time: 15 minutes **Cooking Time:** 15 minutes **Servings:** 4

Ingredients:

For the Sauce
- ½ cup Low-Carb No-Cook Tomato Ketchup (here)
- 2 tablespoons apple cider vinegar
- 1 tablespoon pure maple syrup
- ½ teaspoon freshly ground black pepper
- ½ teaspoon onion powder
- Juice of ½ lemon
- ½ teaspoon Worcestershire sauce
- Freshly ground white pepper

For the Burgers
- 8 ounces lean ground turkey
- 1 celery stalk, finely chopped
- 1 scallion, white and green parts, finely hashed
- 4 whole-wheat dinner rolls, split
- 4 lettuce leaves
- 4 tomato slices

Directions:

To Make the Sauce
1. In a small saucepan, merge the ketchup, vinegar, maple syrup, black pepper, onion powder, lemon juice, Worcestershire sauce, and white pepper, and bring to a simmer over medium heat.
2. Simmer for about 5 minutes until the sauce is thickened. Set aside.

To Make the Burgers
1. In a mixing bowl, combine the turkey, celery, and scallion, and stir well to combine. Form the turkey mixture into 4 small patties.
2. In a grill pan or a cast iron pan over medium-high heat, brown the burgers for about 3 minutes on each side. Using a pastry brush, glaze the tops of the burgers with the barbecue sauce, then flip, and spread sauce on the opposite side. Cook until the juices run clear.
3. Open the dinner rolls and place one burger in each. Top with lettuce and tomato and serve.

Nutrition:
Calories: 213
Fat: 7g
Protein: 15g
Carbohydrates: 26g
Sugars: 11g
Fiber: 4g
Sodium: 276mg

83. Turkey and Quinoa Caprese Casserole

Preparation Time: 10 minutes **Cooking Time:** 35 minutes **Servings:** 8

Ingredients:
- ⅔ cup quinoa
- 1⅓ cups water
- Nonstick cooking spray
- 2 teaspoons extra-virgin olive oil
- 1 pound lean ground turkey
- ¼ cup chopped red onion
- ½ teaspoon salt
- 1 (15-ounce can) fire-roasted tomatoes, drained
- 4 cups spinach leaves, finely sliced
- 3 garlic cloves, minced
- ¼ cup sliced fresh basil
- ¼ cup chicken or vegetable broth
- 2 large ripe tomatoes, sliced
- 4 ounces mozzarella cheese, thinly sliced

Directions:

1. In a small pot, merge the quinoa and water. Set to a boil, reduce the heat, cover, and simmer for 10 minutes. Turn off the heat, and let the quinoa sit for 5 minutes to absorb any remaining water.
2. Preheat the oven to 400F. Set a baking dish with nonstick cooking spray.
3. In a large skillet, warmth the oil over medium heat. Add the turkey, onion, and salt. Cook until the turkey is cooked through and crumbled.
4. Add the tomatoes, spinach, garlic, and basil. Stir in the broth and cooked quinoa. Set the mixture to the prepared baking dish. Arrange the tomato and cheese slices on top.
5. Bake for 15 minutes. Serve.

Nutrition:
Calories: 218
Fat: 9g
Protein: 18g
Carbohydrates: 1.7g
Sugars: 3g
Fiber: 3g
Sodium: 340mg

84. Turkey Divan Casserole

Preparation Time: 10 minutes **Cooking Time:** 50 minutes **Servings:** 6

Ingredients:
- Nonstick cooking spray
- 3 teaspoons extra-virgin olive oil, divided
- 1 pound turkey cutlets
- Pinch salt
- ¼ teaspoon freshly ground black pepper, divided
- ¼ cup chopped onion
- 2 garlic cloves, minced
- 2 tablespoons whole-wheat flour
- 1 cup unsweetened plain almond milk
- 1 cup low-sodium chicken broth
- ½ cup shredded Swiss cheese, divided
- ½ teaspoon dried thyme
- 4 cups chopped broccoli
- ¼ cup coarsely ground almonds

Directions:
1. Preheat the oven to 375F. Set a baking dish with nonstick cooking spray.
2. In a skillet, heat 1 teaspoon of oil over medium heat. Flavor the turkey with the salt and ⅛ teaspoon of pepper. Sauté the turkey cutlets for 5 to 7 minutes on each side until cooked through. Set to a cutting board, cool briefly, and cut into bite-size pieces.
3. In the same pan, warmth the remaining 2 teaspoons of oil over medium-high heat. Sauté the onion for 3 minutes until it begins to soften. Attach the garlic and continue cooking for another minute.
4. Stir in the flour and mix well. Whisk in the almond milk, broth, and remaining ⅛ teaspoon of pepper and continue whisking until smooth. Add ¼ cup of cheese and the thyme and continue stirring until the cheese is melted.
5. In the prepared baking dish, arrange the broccoli on the bottom. Cover with half the sauce. Set the turkey pieces on top of the broccoli, and cover with the remaining sauce. Sprinkle with the remaining ¼ cup of cheese and the ground almonds.
6. Bake for 35 minutes.

Nutrition:
Calories: 207   Carbohydrates: 9g   Sodium: 128mg
Fat: 8g   Sugars: 2g
Protein: 25g   Fiber: 3g

85. Spiced Chicken Breast

Preparation Time: 5 minutes **Cooking Time:** 12 minutes **Servings:** 1

Ingredients:
- ½ tablespoon avocado oil
- ½ teaspoon ground cumin
- ⅛ teaspoon smoked paprika
- Pinch of cayenne pepper
- Salt and ground black pepper, as required
- 1 (4-ounce) boneless, skinless chicken breast

Directions:
1. Preheat the grill to medium-high heat. Grease the grill grate.
2. In a small bowl, attach the oil, spices, salt and black pepper and mix well. Rub the chicken breast with oil mixture evenly.
3. Place the chicken breast onto the grill and cook for about 4-6 minutes per side.
4. Serve hot.

Nutrition:
Calories: 144   Fiber: 0.6g   Sodium: 215mg
Fat: 4   Sugar: 0.1g
Carbohydrates: 1.1g   Protein: 24.4g

86. Seasoned Chicken Breast

Preparation Time: 10 minutes **Cooking Time:** 14 minutes **Servings:** 1

Ingredients:
- 1 tablespoon balsamic vinegar
- ½ tablespoon olive oil
- ¼ teaspoon lemon-pepper seasoning
- 1 (6-ounce) boneless, skinless chicken breast halved, pounded slightly

Directions:
1. In a glass bowl, place the vinegar, oil and seasoning and mix well. Add the chicken breast and coat with the mixture generously. Refrigerate to marinate for about 25-30 minutes.

2. Preheat the grill to medium heat. Grease the grill grate.
3. Remove the chicken breast from bowl and discard the remaining marinade.
4. Place the chicken breast onto the grill and cover with the lid. Cook for about 5-7 minutes per side.
5. Serve immediately.

Nutrition:
Calories: 258
Fat: 10.5g
Carbohydrates: 0.5g
Fiber: 0.1g
Sugar: 0.1g
Protein: 36.1g
Sodium: 88mg

87. Bruschetta Chicken

Preparation Time: 10 minutes **Cooking Time:** 40 minutes **Servings:** 1

Ingredients:
- 1 skinless chicken breast
- Salt and ground black pepper, as required
- 1 small tomato, chopped
- ½ tablespoon fresh basil, chopped
- ¼ of garlic clove, minced
- ¼ teaspoon balsamic vinegar
- ¼ teaspoon olive oil

Directions:
1. Preheat your oven to 375F. Grease a baking dish.
2. Flavor the chicken breast with salt and black pepper evenly.
3. Arrange the chicken breast into the prepared baking dish. Seal the baking dish and bake for approximately 35-40 minutes or until chicken is done completely.
4. Meanwhile, in a bowl, add the tomatoes, basil, garlic, vinegar, oil and salt mix. Refrigerate until using.
5. Remove the baking dish of chicken from oven and transfer the chicken breast onto serving plates. Top with tomato mixture and serve.

Nutrition:
Calories: 297
Fat: 10.5g
Carbohydrates: 3.8g
Fiber: 1.1g
Sugar: 2.3g
Protein: 40.6g
Sodium: 275mg

88. Chicken with Caper Sauce

Preparation Time: 10 minutes **Cooking Time:** 15 minutes **Servings:** 1

Ingredients:
- 2-3 tablespoons almond flour
- Salt, as required
- 1 (5-ounce) skinless, boneless chicken breast half
- ½ tablespoon olive oil
- 2-3 tablespoons low-sodium chicken broth
- 2 teaspoons fresh lemon juice
- 1 tablespoon capers, drained

Directions:
1. In a shallow bowl, merge together the flour and salt. Add the chicken breast and oat with flour mixture evenly. Then, shake off the excess flour.
2. In a small skillet, warmth the oil over medium-high heat and cook the chicken breast. With a slotted spoon, transfer the chicken breast onto a plate and with a piece of foil, cover them to keep warm.
3. In the same skillet, attach the broth and bring to a boil, scraping up the browned bits from the bottom of the pan. Add the lemon juice and cook for about 2-3 minutes or until reduced by half.
4. Remove from the heat and stir in the capers.
5. Place the caper sauce over the chicken breast and serve.

Nutrition:
Calories: 333
Fat: 17.5g
Carbohydrates: 2.3g
Fiber: 1.6g
Sugar: 0.8g
Protein: 31.6g
Sodium: 265mg

89. Yogurt and Parmesan Chicken Bake

Preparation Time: 10 minutes **Cooking Time:** 45 minutes **Servings:** 1

Ingredients:
- 2 tablespoons fat-free plain Greek yogurt
- 1 tablespoon low-fat Parmesan cheese, grated
- Salt and ground black pepper, as required
- 1 (4-ounce) boneless, skinless chicken breast

Directions:

1. Warmth your oven to 375 F. Line baking sheet with a greased piece of foil.
2. In a bowl, add the yogurt, cheese, garlic powder and black pepper and mix well. Add the chicken breast and coat with the yogurt mixture evenly.
3. Arrange the chicken breast onto the prepared baking sheet. Bake for approximately 45 minutes.
4. Serve hot.

Nutrition:
Calories: 156
Fat: 3.5g
Carbohydrates: 2.2g
Fiber: 0g
Sugar: 0g
Protein: 26.3g
Sodium: 285mg

90. Pesto Chicken Bake

Preparation Time: 10 minutes **Cooking Time:** 42 minutes **Servings:** 1

Ingredients:
- 1 (4-ounce) boneless, skinless chicken breast half
- 1 tablespoon basil pesto
- 1 tablespoon part-skim mozzarella cheese, shredded

Directions:
1. Preheat your oven to 400F. Line baking sheet with a greased piece of foil.
2. In a bowl, add the chicken breast and pesto and mix until well combined.
3. Arrange the chicken breast onto the prepared baking sheet in a single layer. Bake for approximately 35 minutes.
4. Remove from the oven and top the chicken breast with the cheese. Bake for approximately 5-7 minutes or until cheese melts completely.
5. Serve hot.

Nutrition:
Calories: 210
Fat: 7.9g
Carbohydrates: 1.1g
Fiber: 0g
Sugar: 0g
Protein: 32.1g
Sodium: 225mg

91. Chicken and Broccoli Bake

Preparation Time: 10 minutes **Cooking Time:** 45 minutes **Servings:** 1

Ingredients:
- 1 (5-ounce) skinless, boneless chicken thigh
- 3 ounces broccoli florets
- 1 garlic clove, minced
- 1 tablespoon extra-virgin olive oil
- ¼ teaspoon dried oregano, crushed
- ¼ teaspoon dried rosemary, crushed
- Salt and ground black pepper, as required

Directions:
1. Preheat your oven to 375F. Grease a small baking dish.
2. In a bowl, attach all the ingredients and toss to coat well.
3. Set the broccoli florets in the bottom of prepared baking dish and top with chicken breast.
4. Bake for approximately 45 minutes.
5. Serve hot.

Nutrition:
Calories: 333
Fat: 17.5g
Carbohydrates: 7.1g
Fiber: 2.6g
Sugar: 1.5g
Protein: 34.3g
Sodium: 235mg

92. Chicken and Veggies Bake

Preparation Time: 10 minutes **Cooking Time:** 45 minutes **Servings:** 1

Ingredients:
- 1 (5-ounce) boneless, skinless chicken thigh
- ¼ teaspoon dried oregano, crushed
- Salt and ground black pepper, as required
- 2 teaspoons olive oil, divided
- 2 fresh mushrooms, sliced
- 1 tablespoon yellow onion, chopped
- 1 small garlic clove, minced
- ¼ cup fresh spinach, chopped
- 1 tablespoon sun-dried tomatoes, sliced
- 1 tablespoon low-fat cheddar cheese, grated

Directions:
1. Preheat your oven to 375F.

2. Season the chicken thigh with the oregano, salt and black pepper evenly.
3. In a small oven-proof skillet, heat 1 teaspoon of oil over medium-high heat and cook the chicken thigh for about 2-3 minutes per side or until browned completely. With a slotted spoon, transfer the chicken thigh onto a plate.
4. In the same skillet, warmth the remaining oil over medium heat and sauté the mushrooms, onions and garlic for about 5-7 minutes.
5. Spill the spinach and sun-dried tomatoes and remove from the heat.
6. Sprinkle with cheese and transfer the skillet into the oven. Bake for 20-30 minutes until desired doneness of chicken.
7. Remove from the oven and set aside for about 5 minutes before serving.

Nutrition:
Calories: 300
Fat: 14.5g
Carbohydrates: 5.1g
Fiber: 1.9g
Sugar: 2g
Protein: 31.8g
Sodium: 265mg

93. Chicken with Olives

Preparation Time: 10 minutes **Cooking Time:** 30 minutes **Servings:** 1

Ingredients:
- 1 boneless, skinless chicken breast
- ¼ tablespoon garlic, minced
- ¼ teaspoon dried oregano, divided
- Salt and ground black pepper, as required
- ¼ cup low-sodium chicken broth
- ½ tablespoon fresh lemon juice
- ¼ cup onion, chopped finely
- ¼ cup tomato, chopped
- 1 tablespoon green olives, pitted and sliced
- 1 teaspoon fresh parsley leaves, chopped

Directions:
1. With a knife, make 3 slits on both sides of each chicken breast. Massage both sides of each breast with garlic, inserting some into the slits. Season the chicken with ½ of the oregano, salt and black pepper evenly.
2. In a small cast iron skillet, heat the oil over medium-high heat and cook for about 5 minutes per side. Stir in the broth, lemon juice and remaining oregano and bring to a gentle boil.
3. Set the heat to medium and cook, covered tightly for about 10-15 minutes, flipping the chicken breast once halfway through.
4. Uncover and place the onions, tomatoes and olives on top. Cook, covered tightly for about 3-5 minutes.
5. Stir in the parsley and serve hot.

Nutrition:
Calories: 201
Fat: 4.5g
Carbohydrates: 6.4g
Fiber: 1.6g
Sugar: 2.6g
Protein: 31.6g
Sodium: 265mg

94. Chicken with Bell Peppers

Preparation Time: 10 minutes **Cooking Time:** 26 minutes **Servings:** 1

Ingredients:
- ½ tablespoon extra-virgin olive oil
- ½ of small onion, chopped
- 1 garlic clove, minced
- ¼ teaspoon fresh ginger, minced
- 1 (4-ounce) skinless, boneless chicken breast, cubed
- 1 small tomato, seeded and chopped
- 1 small bell pepper, seeded and chopped
- ¼ tablespoon fresh lemon juice
- Salt and ground black pepper, as required

Directions:
1. In a skillet, warmth the oil over medium heat and sauté the onion for about 4-5 minutes. Attach the garlic and ginger and sauté for about 1 minute.
2. Add the chicken and cook for about 10 minutes or until browned from all sides. Add the tomato and bell pepper and cook for about 5-7 minutes or until vegetables become tender. Add the lemon juice, salt and black pepper and cook for about 2-3 minutes.
3. Serve hot.

Nutrition:
Calories: 252
Fat: 10.5g
Carbohydrates: 9.1g
Fiber: 3.2g
Sugar: 4.3g
Protein: 27.4g
Sodium: 205mg

95. Chicken with Bok Choy

Preparation Time: 10 minutes **Cooking Time:** 12 minutes **Servings:** 1

Ingredients:
- ½ tablespoon olive oil
- ¼ of onion, sliced thinly
- ¼ teaspoons fresh ginger, grated finely
- 1 small garlic clove, minced
- 2 tablespoons low-sodium chicken broth
- 2 tablespoons fresh orange juice
- ¼ pound cooked chicken, chopped
- ⅓ pound bok choy leaves
- Ground black pepper, as required

Directions:
1. In a small skillet, warmth oil over medium heat and sauté onion for about 3-4 minutes. Add ginger and garlic and sauté for about 1 minute. Add orange zest, broth and orange juice and stir to combine. Add the bok choy and cook for about 1-2 minutes.
2. Add the chicken meat and cook for about 3 minutes. Stir in the black pepper and detach from the heat.
3. Serve hot.

Nutrition:
Calories: 280   Fiber: 2.3g   Sodium: 180mg
Fat: 9.5g   Sugar: 4.3g
Carbohydrates: 8.1g   Protein: 35.6g

96. Chicken with Cabbage

Preparation Time: 10 minutes **Cooking Time:** 15 minutes **Servings:** 1

Ingredients:
- ¾ tablespoon olive oil, divided
- ½ tablespoon apple cider vinegar
- Salt and ground black pepper, as required
- 1 (4-ounce) skinless, boneless chicken breast, sliced thinly
- 1 tablespoon onion, chopped
- ¼ of head cabbage, sliced thinly
- 2 tablespoons water

Directions:
1. In a bowl, mix ¼ tablespoon of oil, vinegar, salt, black pepper, Add the chicken and coat with mixture generously. Set aside for about 5 minutes.
2. Warmth a small non-stick skillet over medium-high heat and stir fry the chicken slices for about 3-4 minutes or until golden brown. Transfer the chicken onto a plate.
3. In the same skillet, melt the remaining oil over medium heat and cook the onion and cabbage for about 4-5 minutes. Attach the chicken and water and cook for about 5-6 minutes or until desired doneness.
4. Serve hot.

Nutrition:
Calories: 22   Fiber: 3.6g   Sodium: 225mg
Fat: 14.5g   Sugar: 4.3g
Carbohydrates: 9.1g   Protein: 27.6g

97. Chicken with Mushrooms

Preparation Time: 10 minutes **Cooking Time:** 18 minutes **Servings:** 1

Ingredients:
- ½ tablespoon olive oil, divided
- 1 (4-ounce) boneless, skinless chicken breast, divided into small pieces
- Salt and ground black pepper, as required
- ⅓ cup fresh mushrooms, sliced
- ¼ cup low-sodium chicken broth

Directions:
1. In a skillet, heat 1 tbsp. of oil over medium-high heat and stir fry the chicken pieces, salt, and black pepper for about 4-5 minutes or until golden-brown. With a slotted spoon, set the chicken pieces onto a plate.
2. In the same skillet, heat the remaining oil over medium heat and sauté the onion, ginger for about 1 minute. Attach the mushrooms and cook for about 6-7 minutes, stirring frequently. Add the cooked chicken and coconut milk and stir fry for about 3 minutes. Attach in the salt and black pepper and remove from the heat.
3. Serve hot.

Nutrition:

Calories: 198	Fiber: 0.2g	Sodium: 235mg
Fat: 9.5g	Sugar: 0.4g	
Carbohydrates: 1g	Protein: 25.1g	

98. Chicken with Broccoli and Mushroom

Preparation Time: 10 minutes **Cooking Time:** 25 minutes **Servings:** 1

Ingredients:
- ½ tablespoon extra-virgin olive oil
- ¼ pound skinless, boneless chicken breast, cubed
- ¼ of small onion, chopped
- 1 garlic clove, minced
- ¼ cup fresh mushrooms, sliced
- ¼ cup small broccoli florets
- 2-3 tablespoons water
- Salt and ground black pepper, as required

Directions:
1. Warmth the oil over medium heat and cook the chicken cubes for about 4-5 minutes. With a slotted spoon, transfer the chicken cubes onto a plate.
2. In the same wok, attach the onion and sauté for about 4-5 minutes. Attach the mushrooms and cook for about 4-5 minutes. Stir in the cooked chicken, broccoli and water and cook, covered for about 8-10 minutes, stirring occasionally.
3. Stir in salt and black pepper and remove from heat.
4. Serve hot.

Nutrition:

Calories: 285	Fiber: 1.2g	Sodium: 205mg
Fat: 17.5g	Sugar: 1.5g	
Carbohydrates: 4g	Protein: 25.6g	

99. Chicken with Zucchini Noodles

Preparation Time: 10 minutes **Cooking Time:** 13 minutes **Servings:** 1

Ingredients:
- 1 small zucchinis, spiralized with Blade C
- Salt, as required
- ¼ teaspoon garlic, minced
- ¼ teaspoon fresh ginger, minced
- 1 (4-ounce) skinless, boneless chicken breast, cubed
- 1 tablespoon fresh orange juice, divided
- ¼ tablespoon fresh lime juice
- 1-2 drops liquid stevia
- ½ teaspoon fresh lime zest, grated finely

Directions:
1. Arrange a strainer over sink. Place the zucchini noodles in a strainer and sprinkle with a pinch of salt. Let the excess moisture release for about 10 minutes. Squeeze the moisture from zucchini and pat dry with paper towels.
2. In a non-stick skillet, warmth oil over medium heat and sauté ginger and garlic for about 1 minute. Stir in chicken and cook for about 4-5 minutes.
3. Add in the remaining ingredients and cook for about 4-5 minutes, stirring occasionally.
4. Attach in zucchini noodles and toss to coat well. Cook for about 1-2 minutes.
5. Serve hot.

Nutrition:

Calories: 171	Fiber: 1.5g	Sodium: 205mg
Fat: 4.3g	Sugar: 3.3g	
Carbohydrates: 6.3g	Protein: 26g	

100. Chicken with Yellow Squash

Preparation Time: 10 minutes **Cooking Time:** 18 minutes **Servings:** 1

Ingredients:
- ½ tablespoon olive oil, divided
- ¼ pound skinless, boneless chicken breast, divided into bite sized pieces
- Salt and ground black pepper, as required
- 1 garlic clove, minced
- ¼ pound yellow squash, sliced
- ¼ tablespoon fresh lemon juice
- ¼ tablespoon fresh parsley, minced

Directions:
1. In a small skillet, warmth ½ tablespoon of oil over medium heat and stir fry chicken for about 6-8 minutes or until golden brown from all sides. Transfer the chicken onto a plate.

2. In the same skillet, warmth remaining oil over medium heat and sauté garlic for about 1 minute. Add squash slices and cook for about 5-6 minutes. Stir in chicken and cook for about 2 minutes.
3. Stir in lemon juice, zest and parsley and remove from heat.
4. Serve hot.

Nutrition:
Calories: 226
Fat: 11g
Carbohydrates: 4.9g
Fiber: 1.4g
Sugar: 2.1g
Protein: 26.9g
Sodium: 206mg

\

Fish and Seafood

101. Salmon Cakes

Preparation Time: 9 minutes **Cooking Time:** 7 minutes **Servings:** 2

Ingredients:
- 8 oz. fresh salmon fillet
- 1 egg
- ⅛ salt
- ¼ garlic powder
- 1 Sliced lemon

Directions:
1. In the bowl, chop the salmon, attach the egg and spices.
2. Form tiny cakes.
3. Let the air fryer preheat to 390F. Set the air fryer bowl of sliced lemons-place cakes on top.
4. Cook them for 7 minutes.

Nutrition:
Calories: 194
Fat: 9g
Carbohydrates: 1g
Proteins: 25g

102. Coconut Shrimp

Preparation Time: 9 minutes **Cooking Time:** 8-10 minutes **Servings:** 4

Ingredients:
- ½ cup pork rinds: ½ cup
- 4 cups jumbo shrimp: 4 cups.

- ½ cup coconut flakes,
- 2 eggs
- ½ cup coconut flour

Dipping sauce:
- 3 tbsp. mayonnaise
- ½ cup sour cream
- ¼ tsp. coconut extract or to taste
- 3 tbsp. coconut cream
- 1 tbsp. olive oil
- Freshly ground black pepper and kosher
- ¼ tsp. pineapple flavoring as much to taste.
- 3 tbsp. coconut flakes preferably unsweetened (optional)

Directions:

Sauce:
1. Merge all the ingredients into a tiny bowl for the dipping sauce (Pineapple flavor). Stir well and put in the fridge until ready to serve.

Shrimps:
1. Spill all eggs in a deep bowl and in a small shallow bowl; attach the hashed pork rinds, coconut flakes, coconut flour, sea salt and ground black pepper.
2. Set the shrimp one by one in the mixed eggs for dipping, then in the coconut flour blend. Set them on a clean plate or put them on your air fryer's basket.
3. Set the shrimp battered in a single layer on your air fryer basket. Drizzle the shrimp with oil and cook for 8 to 10 minutes at 360F, flipping them through halfway.
4. Enjoy hot with dipping sauce.

Nutrition:
Calories: 340
Proteins: 25g
Carbohydrates: 9g
Fat: 16g

103. Crispy Fish Sticks

Preparation Time: 9 minutes **Cooking Time:** 10 minutes **Servings:** 4

Ingredients:
- 1 lb. whitefish such as cod
- ¼ cup mayonnaise
- 2 tbsp. Dijon mustard
- 2 tbsp. water
- 1 ½ cup pork rind
- ¾ tsp. Cajun seasoning
- Kosher salt and pepper to taste
- Cooking spray

Directions:
1. Set with non-stick cooking spray to the air fryer rack.
2. Set the fish dry and cut into sticks about 1 inch by 2 inches' broad
3. Spill together the mayonnaise, mustard, and water in a tiny small dish. Merge the pork rinds and Cajun seasoning into another small container.
4. Operating for one slice of fish at a time, sink to cover in the mayonnaise mix, and then tap off the excess. Dips into the mixture of pork rind, then flip to cover. Set on the rack of an air fryer.
5. Set at 400F to air fry for 5 minutes, then turn the fish with tongs and bake for another 5 minutes. Serve.

Nutrition:
Calories: 263
Fat: 16 g
Carbohydrates: 1 g
Proteins: 26.4 g

104. Honey-Glazed Salmon

Preparation Time: 11 minutes **Cooking Time:** 16 minutes **Servings:** 2

Ingredients:
- 6 tsp. gluten-free soy sauce
- 2 pcs. Salmon fillets
- 3 tsp. sweet rice wine
- 1 tsp. water
- 6 tbsp. honey

Directions:
1. In a bowl, merge sweet rice wine, soy sauce, honey, and water.
2. Set half of it aside.
3. Marinate the fish and keep it rest for 2 hours.
4. Let the air fryer preheat to 180C.
5. Cook the fish, flip halfway through, and cook for another 5 minutes.

6. Set the salmon with marinade mixture after 3 or 4 minutes.
7. The half of marinade pours in a saucepan, reduce to half, and serve with a sauce.

Nutrition:
Calories: 254
Fat: 12g
Carbohydrates: 9.9g
Proteins: 20g

105. Basil-Parmesan Crusted Salmon

Preparation Time: 5 minutes   **Cooking Time:** 7 minutes   **Servings:** 4

Ingredients:
- 3 tbsp. grated Parmesan
- 4 skinless salmon fillets
- ¼ tsp. salt
- Freshly ground black pepper
- 3 tbsp. low-fat mayonnaise
- ¼ cup basil leaves, chopped
- ½ lemon
- Olive oil for spraying

Directions:
1. Let the air fryer preheat to 400F. Spray the basket with olive oil.
2. With salt, pepper, and lemon juice, seasons the salmon.
3. In a bowl, merge 2 tablespoons of Parmesan cheese with mayonnaise and basil leaves.
4. Attach this mix and more parmesan on top of salmon and cook for 7 minutes or until fully cooked.
5. Serve hot.

Nutrition:
Calories: 289
Fat: 18.5g
Carbohydrates: 1.5g
Proteins: 30g

106. Cajun Shrimp

Preparation Time: 9 minutes   **Cooking Time:** 3 minutes   **Servings:** 4

Ingredients:
- 24 extra-jumbo shrimp, peeled,
- 2 tbsp. olive oil
- 1 tbsp. Cajun seasoning
- 1 zucchini, thick slices (half-moons)
- ¼ cup cooked turkey
- 2 yellow squash, sliced half-moons
- ¼ tsp. kosher salt

Directions:
1. In a bowl, merge the shrimp with Cajun seasoning.
2. In another bowl, attach zucchini, turkey, salt, squash, and coat with oil.
3. Let the air fryer preheat to 400F.
4. Set the shrimp and vegetable mix to the fryer basket and cook for 3 minutes.
5. Serve hot.

Nutrition:
Calories: 284
Fat: 14g
Carbohydrates: 8g
Proteins: 31g

107. Crispy Air Fryer Fish

Preparation Time: 11 minutes   **Cooking Time:** 18 minutes   **Servings:** 4

Ingredients:
- 2 tsp. old bay
- 4-6, cut in half, whiting fish fillets
- ¼ cup fine cornmeal
- ¼ cup flour
- 1 tsp. paprika
- ½ tsp. garlic powder
- 1 ½ tsp. salt
- ½ freshly ground black pepper

Directions:
1. In a Ziploc bag, attach all ingredients and coat the fish fillets with it.
2. Set oil on the basket of the air fryer and put the fish in it.
3. Cook for ten minutes at 400F. Flip fish and coat with oil spray and cook for another 7 minutes.
4. Serve with salad green.

Nutrition:
Calories: 254
Fat: 12.7g
Carbohydrates: 8.2g
Proteins: 17.5g

108. Air Fryer Lemon Cod

Preparation Time: 5 minutes **Cooking Time:** 10 minutes **Servings:** 1

Ingredients:
- 1 cod fillet
- 1 tbsp. chopped dried parsley
- Kosher salt and pepper to taste
- 1 tbsp. garlic powder
- 1 lemon

Directions:
1. In a bowl, merge all ingredients and coat the fish fillet with spices.
2. Slice the lemon and set it at the bottom of the air fryer basket.
3. Put spiced fish on top. Cover the fish with lemon slices.
4. Cook for 10 minutes at 375F, the internal temperature of fish should be 145F.
5. Serve.

Nutrition:
Calories: 101
Fat: 1g
Carbohydrates: 10g
Proteins: 16g

109. Salmon Fillets

Preparation Time: 5 minutes **Cooking Time:** 15 minutes **Servings:** 2

Ingredients:
- ¼ cup low-fat Greek yogurt
- 2 salmon fillets
- 1 tbsp. fresh dill (chopped)
- 1 lemon juice
- ½ garlic powder
- Kosher salt and pepper

Directions:
1. Set the lemon into slices and lay it at the bottom of the air fryer basket.
2. Flavor the salmon with kosher salt and pepper. Set salmon on top of lemons.
3. Let it cook at 330F for 15 minutes.
4. In the meantime, merge garlic powder, lemon juice, salt, pepper with yogurt and dill.
5. Serve the fish with sauce.

Nutrition:
Calories: 194
Fat: 7g
Carbohydrates: 6g
Proteins: 25g

110. Fish and Chips

Preparation Time: 11 minutes **Cooking Time:** 35 minutes **Servings:** 4

Ingredients:
- 4 cups any fish fillet
- ¼ cup flour
- 1 cup whole-wheat breadcrumbs
- 1 egg
- 2 tbsp. oil
- 2 potatoes
- 1 tsp. salt

Directions:
1. Cut the potatoes in fries. Then coat with oil and salt.
2. Cook for 20 minutes at 400F, toss the fries halfway through.
3. In the meantime, coat fish in flour, then in the whisked egg, and finally in breadcrumbs mix.
4. Set the fish in the air fryer and let it cook at 330F for 15 minutes.
5. Flip it halfway through, if needed.
6. Serve with tartar sauce and salad green.

Nutrition:
Calories: 409
Fat: 11g
Carbohydrates: 44g
Proteins: 30g

111. Grilled Salmon with Lemon

Preparation Time: 9 minutes **Cooking Time:** 8 minutes **Servings:** 4

Ingredients:
- 2 tbsp. olive oil
- 2 salmon fillets
- ⅓ cup lemon juice
- ⅓ cup water
- ⅓ cup gluten-free light soy sauce
- ⅓ cup honey

- Scallion slices to garnish

Directions:
1. Season salmon with pepper and salt.
2. In a bowl, mix honey, soy sauce, lemon juice, water, oil. Add salmon to this marinade and let it rest for at least 2 hours.

- Freshly ground black pepper, garlic powder, kosher salt to taste

3. Let the air fryer preheat at 180C.
4. Place fish in the air fryer and cook for 8 minutes.
5. Move to a dish and top with scallion slices.

Nutrition:
Calories: 211
Fat: 9g
Carbohydrates: 4.9g
Proteins: 15g

112. Fish Nuggets

Preparation Time: 15 minutes **Cooking Time:** 12 minutes **Servings:** 4

Ingredients:
- 2 cups (skinless) fish fillets in cubes
- 1 egg beaten
- 5 tbsp. flour
- 5 tbsp. water
- Kosher salt and pepper to taste
- ½ cup breadcrumbs mix
- ¼ cup whole-wheat breadcrumbs
- Oil for spraying

Directions:
1. Season the fish cubes with kosher salt and pepper.
2. In a bowl, add flour and gradually add water, mixing as you add.
3. Then mix in the egg. Keep mixing but do not over mix.
4. Coat the cubes in batter, then in the breadcrumb mix. Coat well.
5. Set the cubes in a baking tray and spray with oil.
6. Let the air fryer preheat to 200C.
7. Place cubes in the air fryer and cook for 12 minutes or until well cooked and golden brown.
8. Serve with salad greens.

Nutrition:
Calories: 184
Fat: 3g
Carbohydrates: 10g
Proteins: 19g

113. Garlic Rosemary Grilled Prawns

Preparation Time: 5 minutes **Cooking Time:** 11 minutes **Servings:** 2

Ingredients:
- ½ tbsp. melted butter
- 8 green capsicum slices
- 8 prawns
- ⅛ cup rosemary leaves
- Kosher salt and freshly ground black pepper
- 3-4 cloves minced garlic

Directions:
1. In a bowl, merge all the ingredients and marinate the prawns in it for at least 60 minutes or more.
2. Add 2 prawns and 2 slices of capsicum on each skewer.
3. Let the air fryer preheat to 180C.
4. Cook for 5 to 6 minutes. Then change the temperature to 200C and cook for another 5 minutes.
5. Serve with lemon wedges.

Nutrition:
Calories: 194
Fat: 10g
Carbohydrates: 12g
Proteins: 26g

114. Cajun Catfish

Preparation Time: 5 minutes **Cooking Time:** 15 minutes **Servings:** 4

Ingredients:
- 4 (8 oz.) catfish fillets
- What you'll need from store cupboard:
- 2 tbsp. olive oil
- 2 tsp. garlic salt
- 2 tsp. thyme
- 2 tsp. paprika
- ½ tsp. cayenne pepper
- ½ tsp. red hot sauce
- ¼ tsp. black pepper
- Nonstick cooking spray

Directions:

1. Heat oven to 450F. Set a 9x13-inch baking dish with cooking spray.
2. In a small bowl whisk together everything but catfish. Brush both sides of fillets, using all the spice mix.
3. Bake 10-13 minutes or until fish flakes easily with a fork. Serve.

Nutrition:
Calories: 366
Carbohydrates: 0g
Protein: 35g
Fat: 24g
Sugar: 0g
Fiber: 0g

115. Cajun Flounder and Tomatoes

Preparation Time: 10 minutes **Cooking Time:** 15 minutes **Servings:** 4

Ingredients:
- 4 flounder fillets
- 2 ½ cups tomatoes, diced
- ¾ cup onion, diced
- ¾ cup green bell pepper, diced

What you'll need from store cupboard:
- 2 cloves garlic, diced fine
- 1 tbsp. Cajun seasoning
- 1 tsp. olive oil

Directions:
1. Warmth oil in a large skillet over med-high heat. Add onion and garlic and cook 2 minutes, or until soft.
2. Add tomatoes, peppers and spices, and cook 2-3 minutes until tomatoes soften.
3. Lay fish over top. Seal reduce heat to medium and cook, 5-8 minutes, or until fish flakes easily with fork.
4. Set fish to serving plates and top with sauce.

Nutrition:
Calories: 194
Carbohydrates: 6g
Protein: 32g
Fat: 3g
Sugar: 5g
Fiber: 2g

116. Cajun Shrimp and Roasted Vegetables

Preparation Time: 5 minutes **Cooking Time:** 15 minutes **Servings:** 4

Ingredients:
- 1lb. large shrimp, peeled and deveined
- 2 zucchinis, sliced
- 2 yellow squashes, sliced
- ½ bunch asparagus, cut into thirds
- 2 red bell peppers, cut into chunks

What you'll need from store cupboard:
- 2 tbsp. olive oil
- 2 tbsp. Cajun Seasoning
- Salt and pepper, to taste

Directions:
1. Heat oven to 400F.
2. Merge shrimp and vegetables in a large bowl. Add oil and seasoning and toss to coat.
3. Spread evenly in a large baking sheet and bake 15-2 minutes, or until vegetables are tender.
4. Serve.

Nutrition:
Calories: 251
Carbohydrates: 1.3g
Protein: 30g
Fat: 9g
Sugar: 6g
Fiber: 4g

117. Cilantro Lime Grilled Shrimp

Preparation Time: 5 minutes **Cooking Time:** 5 minutes **Servings:** 6

Ingredients:
- ½ lbs. large shrimp raw, peeled, deveined with tails on
- Juice and zest of 1 lime
- 2 tbsp. fresh cilantro chopped
- ¼ cup olive oil
- 2 cloves garlic, diced fine
- 1 tsp. smoked paprika
- ¼ tsp. cumin
- ½ teaspoon salt
- ¼ tsp. cayenne pepper

Directions:
1. Set the shrimp in a large Ziploc bag.
2. Mix remaining Ingredients in a small bowl and pour over shrimp. Let marinate 20-30 minutes.
3. Heat up the grill and cook the shrimp 2-3 minutes per side, just until they turn pick. Be careful not overcook them. Serve garnished with cilantro.

Nutrition:
- Calories: 317
- Carbohydrates: 4g
- Protein: 39g
- Fat: 15g
- Sugar: 0g
- Fiber: 0g

118. Crab Frittata

Preparation Time: 10 minutes **Cooking Time:** 50 minutes **Servings:** 4

Ingredients:
- 4 eggs
- 2 cups lump crabmeat
- 1 cup half-n-half
- cup green onions, diced
- 1 cup reduced fat parmesan cheese, grated
- ½ tsp. salt
- ½ tsp. pepper
- 1 tsp. smoked paprika
- 1 tsp. Italian seasoning
- Nonstick cooking spray

Directions:
1. Heat oven to 35F. Spray an 8-inch spring form pan, or pie plate with cooking spray.
2. In a large bowl, whisk together the eggs and half-n-half. Add seasonings and parmesan cheese, stir to mix.
3. Stir in the onions and crab meat. Spill into prepared pan and bake 35-40 minutes, or eggs are set and top is lightly browned.
4. Let and then slice and serve warm or at room temperature.

Nutrition:
Calories: 276 Protein: 25g Sugar: 1g
Carbohydrates: 5g Fat: 17g Fiber: 1g

119. Crunchy Lemon Shrimp

Preparation Time: 5 minutes **Cooking Time:** 10 minutes **Servings:** 4

Ingredients:
- 1 lb. raw shrimp, peeled and deveined
- 2 tbsp. Italian parsley, roughly chopped
- 2 tbsp. lemon juice, divided
- ⅔ cup panko breadcrumbs
- 2½ tbsp. olive oil, divided
- Salt and pepper, to taste

Directions:
1. Heat oven to 400F.
2. Set the shrimp evenly in a baking dish and sprinkle with salt and pepper.
3. Drizzle on 1 tbsp. lemon juice and 1 tbsp. of olive oil. Set aside.
4. In a medium bowl, combine parsley, remaining lemon juice, breadcrumbs, remaining olive oil, and 1 tsp. each of salt and pepper. Set the panko mixture evenly on top of the shrimp.
5. Bake 8-10 minutes or until shrimp are cooked through and the panko is golden brown.

Nutrition:
Calories: 283 Protein: 28g Sugar: 1g
Carbohydrates: 1.5g Fat: 12g Fiber: 1g

120. Grilled Tuna Steaks

Preparation Time: 5 minutes **Cooking Time:** 10 minutes **Servings:** 6

Ingredients:
- 6 6 oz. tuna steaks
- 3 tbsp. fresh basil, diced
- 4 ½ tsp. olive oil
- ¾ tsp. salt
- ¼ tsp. pepper
- Nonstick cooking spray

Directions:
1. Heat grill to medium heat. Spray rack with cooking spray.
2. Drizzle both sides of the tuna with oil. Sprinkle with basil, salt and pepper.
3. Place on grill and cook 5 minutes per side, tuna should be slightly pink in the center.
4. Serve.

Nutrition:
Calories: 343 Protein: 51g Sugar: 0g
Carbohydrates: 0g Fat: 14g Fiber: 0g

Veggies

121. Baked Zucchini Recipe from Mexico

Preparation Time: 10 minutes **Cooking Time:** 30 minutes **Servings:** 4

Ingredients:

- 1 tablespoon olive oil
- 1-½ pounds' zucchini, cubed
- ½ cup chopped onion
- ½ teaspoon garlic salt
- ½ teaspoon paprika
- ½ teaspoon dried oregano
- ½ teaspoon cayenne pepper
- ½ cup cooked long-grain rice

- ½ cup cooked pinto beans
- 1-¼ cups salsa

Directions:
1. Set the baking pan of air fryer with olive oil. Add onions and zucchini and for 10 minutes, cook on 360F. Halfway through cooking time, stir.
2. Season with cayenne, oregano, paprika, and garlic salt. Mix well.

- ¾ cup shredded Cheddar cheese

3. Stir in salsa, beans, and rice. Cook for 5 minutes.
4. Stir in cheddar cheese and mix well.
5. Cover pan with foil.
6. Cook for 15 minutes at 390F until bubbly.
7. Serve and enjoy.

Nutrition:
Calories: 263
Carbohydrates: 24.6g
Protein: 12.5g
Fat: 12.7g

122. Banana Pepper Stuffed with Tofu 'n Spices

Preparation Time: 5 minutes **Cooking Time:** 10 minutes **Servings:** 8

Ingredients:
- ½ teaspoon red chili powder
- ½ teaspoon turmeric powder
- 1 onion, finely chopped
- 1 package firm tofu, crumbled
- 1 teaspoon coriander powder
- 3 tablespoons coconut oil
- 8 banana peppers, top end sliced and seeded
- Salt to taste

Directions:
1. Preheat the air fryer for 5 minutes.
2. In a mixing bowl, combine the tofu, onion, coconut oil, turmeric powder, red chili powder, coriander power, and salt. Mix until well-combined.
3. Scoop the tofu mixture into the hollows of the banana peppers.
4. Place the stuffed peppers in the air fryer.
5. Close and cook for 10 minutes at 3250F.

Nutrition:
Calories: 72
Carbohydrates: 4.1g
Protein: 1.2g
Fat: 5.6

123. Baked Potato Topped with Cream cheese 'n Olives

Preparation Time: 15 minutes **Cooking Time:** 40 minutes **Servings:** 1

Ingredients:
- ¼ teaspoon onion powder
- 1 medium russet potato, scrubbed and peeled
- 1 tablespoon chives, chopped
- 1 tablespoon Kalamata olives
- 1 teaspoon olive oil
- ⅛ teaspoon salt
- a dollop of vegan butter
- a dollop of vegan cream cheese

Directions:
1. Place inside the air fryer basket and cook for 40 minutes. Be sure to turn the potatoes once halfway.
2. Set the potatoes in a bowl and pour in olive oil, onion powder, salt, and vegan butter.
3. Preheat the air fryer to 400F.
4. Serve the potatoes with vegan cream cheese, Kalamata olives, chives, and other vegan toppings that you want.

Nutrition:
Calories: 504
Carbohydrates: 68.34g
Protein: 9.31g
Fat: 21.53g

124. Brussels sprouts with Balsamic Oil

Preparation Time: 5 minutes **Cooking Time:** 15 minutes **Servings:** 4

Ingredients:
- ¼ teaspoon salt
- 1 tablespoon balsamic vinegar
- 2 cups Brussels sprouts, halved
- 2 tablespoons olive oil

Directions:
1. Preheat the air fryer for 5 minutes.
2. Mix all ingredients in a bowl until the zucchini fries are well coated.
3. Place in the air fryer basket.
4. Close and cook for 15 minutes for 350F.

Nutrition:
Calories: 82
Carbohydrates: 4.6g
Protein: 1.5g
Fat: 6.8g

125. Bell Pepper-Corn Wrapped in Tortilla

Preparation Time: 5 minutes **Cooking Time:** 15 minutes **Servings:** 4

Ingredients:
- 1 small red bell pepper, chopped
- 1 small yellow onion, diced
- 1 tablespoon water
- 2 cobs grilled corn kernels
- 4 large tortillas
- 4 pieces' commercial vegan nuggets, chopped
- mixed greens for garnish

Directions:
1. Preheat the air fryer to 400F.
2. In a skillet heated over medium heat, water sauté the vegan nuggets together with the onions, bell peppers, and corn kernels. Set aside.
3. Place filling inside the corn tortillas.
4. Fold the tortillas and place inside the air fryer and cook for 15 minutes until the tortilla wraps are crispy.
5. Serve with mix greens on top.

Nutrition:
Calories: 548
Carbohydrates: 43.54g
Protein: 46.73g
Fat: 20.76g

126. Black Bean Burger with Garlic-Chipotle

Preparation Time: 10 minutes **Cooking Time:** 20 minutes **Servings:** 3

Ingredients:
- ½ cup corn kernels
- ½ teaspoon chipotle powder
- ½ teaspoon garlic powder
- ¾ cup salsa
- 1 ¼ teaspoon chili powder
- 1 ½ cup rolled oats
- 1 can black beans, rinsed and drained
- 1 tablespoon soy sauce

Directions:
1. In a mixing bowl, merge all Ingredients and mix using your hands.
2. Form small patties using your hands and set aside.
3. Brush patties with oil if desired.
4. Place the grill pan in the air fryer and place the patties on the grill pan accessory.
5. Seal the lid and cook for 20 minutes on each side at 330F.

Nutrition:
Calories: 395
Carbohydrates: 52.2g
Protein: 24.3g
Fat: 5.8g

127. Vegan Edamame Quinoa Collard Wraps

Preparation Time: 5 minutes **Cooking Time:** 15 minutes **Servings:** 4

Ingredients:

For the wrap:
- 2 to 3 Collard leaves.
- ¼ cup Grated carrot
- ¼ cup Sliced cucumber
- ¼ thin strips red bell pepper.
- ¼ thin strips orange bell pepper.
- ⅓ cup cooked quinoa.
- ⅓ cup Shelled defrosted edamame

For the dressing:
- Fresh ginger root; 3 tablespoons; peeled and chopped
- Cooked chickpeas; 1 cup
- Clove of garlic; 1
- Rice vinegar; 4 tablespoons
- Low sodium tamari/coconut aminos; 2 tablespoons
- Lime juice; 2 tablespoons
- Water; ¼ cup
- Few pinches of chili flakes
- Stevia; 1 pack

Directions:
1. For the dressing, merge all the ingredients and purée in a food processor until smooth.
2. Load into a little jar or tub and set aside.
3. Place the collar leaves on a flat surface, covering one another to create a tighter tie.
4. Take one tablespoon of ginger dressing and blend it up with the prepared quinoa.

5. Spoon the prepared quinoa onto the leaves and shape a simple horizontal line at the closest end.
6. Supplement the edamame with all the veggie fillings left over.
7. Drizzle around one tablespoon of the ginger dressing on top, then fold the cover's sides inwards.
8. Pullover the fillings, the side of the cover closest to you, then turn the whole body away to seal it up.

Nutrition:
Calories: 295
Sugar: 3 g
Sodium: 200 mg
Fat: 13 g

128. Baked Eggplant with Marinara

Preparation Time: 20 minutes **Cooking Time:** 45 minutes **Servings:** 3

Ingredients:
- 1 clove garlic, sliced
- 1 large eggplants
- 1 tablespoon olive oil
- 1 tablespoon olive oil
- ½ pinch salt, or as needed
- ¼ cup and 2 tbsp. dry breadcrumbs
- ¼ cup and 2 tablespoons ricotta cheese
- ¼ cup grated Parmesan cheese
- ¼ cup grated Parmesan cheese
- ¼ cup water, plus as needed
- ¼ teaspoon red pepper flakes
- 1-½ cups prepared marinara sauce
- 1-½ teaspoons olive oil
- 2 tablespoons shredded pepper jack cheese
- salt and freshly ground black pepper

Directions:
1. Cut the eggplant crosswise into 5 pieces. Peel a pumpkin, grate it and cut it into two cubes.
2. Lightly turn skillet with 1 Tbsp. olive oil. Heat the oil at 390F for 5 minutes. Add half of the aubergines and cook 2 minutes on each side. Transfer to a plate.
3. Add 1 tbsp. of olive oil and add garlic. Cook for one minute. Add the chopped aubergines. Season with pepper flakes and salt. Cook for 4 minutes. Lower the heat to 330F and continue cooking the eggplants until soft, about 8 more minutes.
4. Stir in water and marinara sauce. Cook for 7 minutes until heated through. Stirring every now and then. Transfer to a bowl.
5. In a bowl, whisk well pepper, salt, pepper jack cheese, Parmesan cheese, and ricotta. Evenly spread cheese over eggplant strips and then fold in half.
6. Lay folded eggplant in baking pan. Pour marinara sauce on top.
7. In a small bowl whisk well olive oil, and breadcrumbs. Sprinkle all over sauce.
8. Cook for 15 minutes at 390F until tops are lightly browned.
9. Serve and enjoy.

Nutrition
Calories: 405
Carbohydrates: 41.1g
Protein: 12.7g
Fat: 21.4g

129. Crispy-Topped Baked Vegetables

Preparation Time: 10 minutes **Cooking Time:** 40 minutes **Servings:** 4

Ingredients:
- 2 tbsp. olive oil
- 1 onion, chopped
- 1 celery stalk, chopped
- 2 carrots, grated
- ½-pound turnips, sliced
- 1 cup vegetable broth
- 1 tsp. turmeric
- Sea salt and black pepper, to taste
- ½ tsp. liquid smoke
- 1 cup Parmesan cheese, shredded
- 2 tbsp. fresh chives, chopped

Directions:
1. Set oven to 360F and grease a baking dish with olive oil.
2. Set a skillet with medium heat and warm olive oil.
3. Sweat the onion until soft, and place in the turnips, carrots, and celery; and cook for 4 minutes.
4. Remove the vegetable mixture to the baking dish.
5. Combine vegetable broth with turmeric, pepper, liquid smoke, and salt.
6. Spread this mixture over the vegetables.
7. Sprinkle with Parmesan cheese and bake for about minutes.
8. Garnish with chives to serve.

Nutrition:

Calories: 242

Fats: 16.3 g

Carbohydrates: 8.6 g

Protein: 16.3 g

130. Creamy Spinach and Mushroom Lasagna

Preparation Time: 60 minutes **Cooking Time:** 20 minutes **Servings:** 6

Ingredients:

- 10 lasagna noodles
- 1 package whole milk ricotta
- 2 packages of frozen chopped spinach.
- 4 cups mozzarella cheese (divided and shredded)

For the Sauce:

- ¼ cup of butter (unsalted)
- 2 cloves garlic
- 1 pound of thinly sliced cremini mushroom
- 1 diced onion
- ¼ cup flour
- ¾ cup grated fresh Parmesan
- 3 tablespoons chopped fresh parsley leaves (optional)
- 4 cups milk, kept at room temperature
- 1 teaspoon basil (dried)
- Pinch of nutmeg
- Salt and freshly ground black pepper

Directions:

1. Preheat oven to 352F.
2. To make the sauce, over a medium heat, melt your butter. Add garlic, mushrooms, and onion. Cook and stir at intervals until it becomes tender at about 3-4 minutes.
3. Whisk in flour until lightly browned, it takes about 1 minute for it to become brown.
4. Next, whisk in the milk gradually, and cook, constantly whisking, about 2-3 minutes till it becomes thickened. Stir in basil, oregano, and nutmeg, season with salt and pepper for taste.
5. Then set aside.
6. In another set of pot of boiling salted water, cook lasagna noodles according to the package instructions.
7. Spread one cup mushroom sauce onto the bottom of a baking dish; top it with four lasagna noodles, ½ of the spinach, one cup mozzarella cheese, and ¼ cup Parmesan.
8. Repeat this process with remaining noodles, mushroom sauce, and cheeses.
9. Place into oven and bake for 35-45 minutes, or until it starts bubbling. Then boil for 2-3 minutes until it becomes brown and translucent.
10. Let cool for 15 minutes.
11. Serve it with garnished parsley (optional)

Nutrition:

Calories: 488.3

Fats: 19.3 g

Cholesterol: 88.4 mg

Sodium: 451.9 mg

Carbohydrates: 51.0 g

Protein: 25.0 g

131. Zucchini Parmesan Chips

Preparation Time: 5 minutes **Cooking Time:** 8 minutes **Servings:** 10

Ingredients:

- ½ tsp. paprika
- ½ C. grated parmesan cheese
- ½ C. Italian breadcrumbs
- 1 lightly beaten egg
- 1 thinly sliced zucchinis

Directions:

1. Use a very sharp knife or mandolin slicer to slice zucchini as thinly as you can. Pat off extra moisture.
2. Beat egg with a pinch of pepper and salt and a bit of water.
3. Combine paprika, cheese, and breadcrumbs in a bowl.
4. Dip slices of zucchini into the egg mixture and then into breadcrumb mixture. Press gently to coat.
5. With olive oil cooking spray, mist coated zucchini slices. Place into your air fryer in a single layer.
6. Cook 8 minutes at 350F.
7. Sprinkle with salt and serve with salsa.

Nutrition:
Calories: 211
Fat: 16g
Protein: 8g
Sugar: 0g

132. Roasted Squash Puree
Preparation Time: 20 minutes **Cooking Time:** 6 to 7 hours **Servings:** 8

Ingredients:
- 1 (3-pound) butternut squash, skinned, seeded, and cut into 1-inch pieces
- 3 (1-pound) acorn squash, peeled, seeded, and cut into 1-inch pieces
- 2 onions, chopped
- 3 garlic cloves, minced
- 2 tablespoons olive oil
- 1 teaspoon dried marjoram leaves
- ½ teaspoon salt
- ⅛ teaspoon freshly ground black pepper

Directions:
1. In a 6-quart slow cooker, mix all the ingredients.
2. Seal and cook on low for 6 to 7 hours, or until the squash is tender when pierced with a fork.
3. Smash the squash right in the slow cooker.

Nutrition:
Calories: 175
Carbohydrates: 38 g
Sugar: 1 g
Fiber: 3 g
Fat: 4 g
Saturated Fat: 1 g
Protein: 3 g
Sodium: 149 mg

133. Roasted Root Vegetables
Preparation Time: 20 minutes **Cooking Time:** 6 to 8 hours **Servings:** 8

Ingredients:
- 6 carrots, cut into 1-inch chunks
- 2 yellow onions, cut into 8 wedges
- 2 sweet potatoes, skinned and cut into chunks
- 6 Yukon Gold skinned, cut into chunks
- 8 whole garlic cloves, peeled
- 4 parsnips, peeled and cut into chunks
- 3 tablespoons olive oil
- 1 teaspoon dried thyme leaves
- ½ teaspoon salt
- ⅛ teaspoon freshly ground black pepper

Directions:
1. In a 6-quart slow cooker, mix all the ingredients.
2. Seal and cook on low for 6 to 8 hours, or until the vegetables are tender.
3. Serve and enjoy!

Nutrition:
Calories: 214
Carbohydrates: 40 g
Sugar: 7 g
Fiber: 6 g
Fat: 5 g
Saturated Fat: 1 g
Protein: 4 g
Sodium: 201 mg

134. Hummus
Preparation Time: 10 minutes **Cooking Time:** 10 minutes **Servings:** 32

Ingredients:
- 4 cups of cooked garbanzo beans
- 1 cup of water
- 1½ tablespoons of lemon juice
- 2 teaspoons of ground cumin
- 1½ teaspoon of ground coriander.
- 1 teaspoon of finely chopped garlic
- ½ teaspoon of salt
- ¼ teaspoon of fresh ground pepper
- Paprika for garnish

Directions:
1. On a food processor, place together the garbanzo beans, lemon juice, water, garlic, salt, and pepper and process it until it becomes smooth and creamy.
2. To achieve your desired consistency, add more water
3. Then spoon out the hummus in a serving bowl
4. Sprinkle your paprika and serve.

Nutrition:
Protein: 0.7 g
Carbohydrates: 2.5 g
Sugars: 0 g
Fat: 1.7 g

135. Thai Roasted Veggies

Preparation Time: 20 minutes **Cooking Time:** 6 to 8 hours **Servings:** 8

Ingredients:
- 4 large carrots, peeled and cut into chunks
- 2 onions, peeled and sliced
- 6 garlic cloves, peeled and sliced
- 2 parsnips, peeled and sliced
- 2 jalapeño peppers, minced
- ½ cup Roasted Vegetable Broth
- ⅓ cup canned coconut milk
- 3 tablespoons lime juice
- 2 tablespoons grated fresh ginger root
- 2 teaspoons curry powder

Directions:
1. In a 6-quart slow cooker, mix the carrots, onions, garlic, parsnips, and jalapeño peppers.
2. In a small bowl, mix the vegetable broth, coconut milk, lime juice, ginger root, and curry powder until well blended. Pour this mixture into the slow cooker.
3. Seal and cook on low for 6 to 8 hours, do it until the vegetables are tender when pierced with a fork.

Nutrition:
Calories: 69 Fiber: 3 g Protein: 1g
Carbohydrates: 13 g Fat: 3g Sodium: 95mg
Sugar: 6 g Saturated Fat: 3g

136. Cheesy Cauliflower Fritters

Preparation Time: 5 minutes **Cooking Time:** 14 minutes **Servings:** 8

Ingredients:
- ½ Cup chopped parsley
- 1 Cup Italian breadcrumbs
- ⅓ Cup shredded mozzarella cheese
- ⅓ Cup shredded sharp cheddar cheese
- 1 egg
- 1 minced garlic cloves
- 1 chopped scallions
- 1 head of cauliflower

Directions:
1. Cut cauliflower up into florets. Wash well and pat dry. Place into a food processor and pulse 20-30 seconds till it looks like rice.
2. Place cauliflower rice in a bowl and mix with pepper, salt, egg, cheeses, breadcrumbs, garlic, and scallions.
3. With hands, form 15 patties of the mixture. Add more breadcrumbs if needed.
4. With olive oil, spritz patties, and place into your air fryer in a single layer.
5. Cook 14 minutes at 390F, flipping after 7 minutes.

Nutrition:
Calories: 209 Protein: 6g
Fat: 17g Sugar: 0.5g

137. Crispy Jalapeno Coins

Preparation Time: 10 minutes **Cooking Time:** 10 minutes **Servings:** 8 to 10

Ingredients:
- 1 egg
- 2-3 tbsp. coconut flour
- 1 sliced and seeded jalapeno
- Pinch of garlic powder
- Pinch of onion powder
- Pinch of Cajun seasoning (optional)
- Pinch of pepper and salt

Directions:
1. Ensure your air fryer is preheated to 400F.
2. Mix all dry ingredients.
3. Pat jalapeno slices dry. Dip coins into egg wash and then into dry mixture. Toss to coat thoroughly.
4. Add coated jalapeno slices to air fryer in a singular layer. Spray with olive oil.
5. Cook just till crispy.

Nutrition:
Calories: 128 Sugar: 0g
Fat: 8g
Protein: 7g

138. Jicama Fries

Preparation Time: 10 minutes **Cooking Time:** 20 minutes **Servings:** 8

Ingredients:
- 1 tbsp. dried thyme
- ¾ Cup arrowroot flour
- ½ large Jicama
- 3 eggs

Directions:
1. Sliced jicama into fries.
2. Whisk eggs together and pour over fries. Toss to coat.
3. Mix a pinch of salt, thyme, and arrowroot flour together. Toss egg-coated jicama into dry mixture, tossing to coat well.
4. Set the air fryer basket with olive oil and add fries. Cook 20 minutes on CHIPS setting. Toss halfway into the cooking process.

Nutrition:
Calories: 211
Fat: 19g
Protein: 9g
Sugar: 1g

139. Air Fryer Brussels sprouts

Preparation Time: 5 minutes **Cooking Time:** 10 minutes **Servings:** 5

Ingredients:
- ¼ tsp. salt
- 1 tbsp. balsamic vinegar
- 1 tbsp. olive oil
- 1 Cup Brussels sprouts

Directions:
1. Cut Brussels sprouts in half lengthwise. Toss with salt, vinegar, and olive oil till coated thoroughly.
2. Add coated sprouts to air fryer, cooking 8-10 minutes at 400 F. Shake after 5 minutes of cooking.
3. Brussels sprouts are ready to devour when brown and crisp!

Nutrition:
Calories: 118
Fat: 9g
Protein: 11g
Sugar: 1g

140. Spaghetti Squash Tots

Preparation Time: 5 minutes **Cooking Time:** 15 minutes **Servings:** 8 to 10

Ingredients:
- ¼ tsp. pepper
- ½ tsp. salt
- 1 thinly sliced scallion
- 1 spaghetti squash

Directions:
1. Rinse and cut the squash in half lengthwise. Scrape out the seeds.
2. With a fork, remove spaghetti meat by strands and throw out skins.
3. In a clean towel, toss in squash and wring out as much moisture as possible. Place in a bowl and with a knife slice through meat a few times to cut smaller.
4. Add pepper, salt, and scallions to squash and mix well.
5. Create "tot" shapes with your hands and place in fryer. Spray with olive oil.
6. Cook 15 minutes at 350 F until golden and crispy!

Nutrition:
Calories: 231
Fat: 18g
Protein: 5g
Sugar: 0g

Snacks

141. Chicken and Mushrooms

Preparation Time: 10 minutes **Cooking Time:** 15 minutes **Servings:** 6

Ingredients:
- 2 chicken breasts
- 1 cup of sliced white champignons
- 1 cup of sliced green chilies
- ½ cup scallions hacked
- 1 teaspoon of chopped garlic
- 1 cup of low-fat cheddar shredded cheese (1-1.5 lb. grams fat / ounce)
- 1 tablespoon of olive oil
- 1 tablespoon of butter

Directions:
1. Fry the chicken breasts with olive oil.
2. When needed, salt and pepper.
3. Grill breasts of chicken in a plate with grill.
4. For every serving, weigh 4 ounces of chicken. (Make two servings, save leftovers for another meal).
5. In a butter pan, stir in mushrooms, green peppers, scallions, and garlic until smooth, and a little dark.
6. Place the chicken in a baking platter.
7. Cover with mushroom combination.
8. Top on ham.
9. Place the cheese in a 350 oven until it melts.

Nutrition:
Carbohydrates: 2 g Fat: 11 g Sodium: 198 mg
Protein: 23 g Cholesterol: 112 mg Potassium: 261 mg

142. Cheeseburger Pie

Preparation Time: 20 minutes **Cooking Time:** 90 minutes **Servings:** 4

Ingredients:
- 1 large spaghetti squash
- 1 lb. lean ground beef
- ¼ cup diced onion
- 2 eggs
- ⅓ cup low-fat, plain Greek yogurt
- 2 tbsp. tomato sauce
- ½ tsp. Worcestershire sauce
- ⅔ cup reduced-fat, shredded cheddar cheese
- 2 oz. dill pickle slices
- Cooking spray

Directions:
1. Preheat oven to 400F. Slice spaghetti squash in half lengthwise; dismiss pulp and seeds.
2. Spray insides with cooking spray.
3. Place squash halves cut-side-down onto a foil-lined baking sheet and bake for 30 minutes.
4. Once cooked, let cool to before scraping squash flesh with a fork to remove spaghetti-like strands; set aside.
5. Push squash strands in the bottom and up sides of the greased pie pan, creating an even layer.
6. Meanwhile, set up pie filling.
7. With a medium-sized skillet, cook beef and onion over medium heat 8 to 10 minutes, sometime stirring, until meat is brown.
8. Drain and remove from heat.
9. In a medium-sized bowl, whisk together eggs, tomat paste, Greek yogurt, and Worcestershire sauce. Sp in ground beef mixture.
10. Set pie filling over squash crust.
11. Drizzle meat filling with cheese, and then top wit dill pickle slices.
12. Bake for 40 minutes.

Nutrition:
Calories: 409
Fat: 24.49 g
Carbohydrates: 15.06 g
Protein: 30.69 g

143. Salmon Feta and Pesto Wrap

Preparation Time: 15 minutes **Cooking Time:** 10 minutes **Servings:** 4

Ingredients:
- 8 ounces (250 g) smoked salmon fillet, thinly sliced
- 1 cup (150 g) feta cheese
- 8 (15 g) Romaine lettuce leaves
- 4 (6-inch) pita bread
- ¼ cup (60 g) basil pesto sauce

Directions:
1. Place 1 pita bread on a plate. Top with lettuce, salmon, feta cheese, and pesto sauce. Fold or roll to enclose filling. Repeat procedure for the remainir ingredients.
2. Serve and enjoy.

Nutrition:
Calories: 379
Fat 17.7 g
Carbohydrates: 36.6 g
Protein: 18.4 g
Sodium: 554 mg

144. Salmon Cream Cheese and Onion on Bagel

Preparation Time: 15 minutes **Cooking Time:** 10 minutes **Servings:** 4

Ingredients:
- 8 ounces (250 g) smoked salmon fillet, thinly sliced
- ½ cup (125 g) cream cheese
- 1 medium (110 g) onion, thinly sliced
- 4 bagels (about 80g each), split
- 2 tablespoons (7 g) fresh parsley, chopped
- Freshly ground black pepper, to taste

Directions:
1. Spread the cream cheese on each bottom's half of bagels. Top with salmon and onion, season with pepper, sprinkle with parsley and then cover wi bagel tops.
2. Serve and enjoy.

Nutrition:
Calories: 309
Fat 14.1 g
Carbohydrates 32.0 g
Protein 14.7 g
Sodium 571 mg

145. Melon Cucumber Salad

Preparation Time: 2 minutes   **Cooking Time:** 3 minutes   **Servings:** 5

Ingredients:
- ¼ cup of finely hashed sweet onion like Vidalia
- ⅓ cup of white balsamic vinegar see note
- 2 garlic cloves finely minced
- kosher salt
- freshly ground black pepper
- 1 lime
- 1 medium melon honeydew, cantaloupe, Crenshaw, canary, etc., cut into rounds with a melon baller
- 1 12-inch English or hothouse cucumber, sliced
- 2 tablespoons of extra virgin olive oil

Directions:
1. Peel the lime and then squeeze it.
2. In a bowl, mix the melon balls, onion, cucumber, and lime zest.

Making the dressing:
1. Add the garlic cloves, lime juice, salt, and pepper.
2. Whisk until well combined. Continue whisking and spill in the olive oil in a steady stream.
3. Spill the dressing over the melon mixture and stir to coat.
4. Let stand; refrigerate until ready to serve.

Nutrition:
Calories: 88.4
Fat: 7.6 g
Carbohydrates: 3.9 g
Protein: 2.5 g

146. Greek Baklava

Preparation Time: 20 minutes   **Cooking Time:** 20 minutes   **Servings:** 18

Ingredients:
- 1 (16 oz.) package phyllo dough
- 1 lb. chopped nuts
- 1 cup butter
- 1 teaspoon ground cinnamon
- 1 cup water
- 1 teaspoon. vanilla extract
- ½ cup honey

Directions:
1. Preheat the oven to 175C or 350F. Set butter on the sides and bottom of a 9-in by 13-in pan.
2. Chop the nuts then mix with cinnamon; set it aside. Unfurl the phyllo dough then halve the whole stack to fit the pan. Use a damp cloth to cover the phyllo to prevent drying as you proceed. Put two phyllo sheets in the pan then butter well. Repeat to make eight layered phyllo sheets. Scatter 2-3 tablespoons. nut mixture over the sheets then places two more phyllo sheets on top, butter then sprinkle with nuts. Layer as you go. The final layer should be six to eight phyllo sheets deep.
3. Make square or diamond shapes with a sharp knife up to the bottom of pan. You can slice into four long rows for diagonal shapes. Bake until crisp and golden for 50 minutes.
4. Meanwhile, boil water and melts to make the sauce; mix in honey and vanilla. Let it simmer for 20 minutes.
5. Take off the baklava out of the oven then drizzle with sauce right away; cool. Serve the baklava in cupcake papers. You can also freeze them without cover. The baklava will turn soggy when wrapped.

Nutrition:
Calories: 393
Carbohydrates: 37.5 g
Cholesterol: 27 mg
Total Fat: 25.9 g
Protein: 6.1 g
Sodium: 196 mg

147. Glazed Bananas in Phyllo Nut Cups

Preparation Time: 30 minutes   **Cooking Time:** 45 minutes   **Servings:** 6 servings.

Ingredients:
- ¾ cup shelled pistachios
- 1 teaspoon. ground cinnamon

Sauce:
- ¾ cup butter, cubed
- 3 medium firm bananas, sliced
- 4 sheets phyllo dough, (14 inches x 9 inches)
- ¼ cup butter, melted
- ¼ teaspoon. ground cinnamon
- 3 to 4 cups vanilla ice cream

Directions:
1. Finely chop pistachios in a food processor; move to a bowl then mix in cinnamon. Slice each phyllo sheet to 6 four-inch squares, get rid of the trimmings. Pile the squares then use plastic wrap to cover.

2. Slather melted butter on each square one at a time then scatter a heaping tablespoonful of pistachio mixture. Pile 3 squares; flip each at an angle to misalign the corners. Force each stack on the sides and bottom of an oiled eight-oz. custard cup. Bake for 15-20 minutes in a 350F oven until golden; cool for 5 minutes. Set to a wire rack to completely cool.
3. Melt and boil butter in a saucepan to make the sauce lower heat. Mix in cinnamon and bananas gently heat completely. Put ice cream in the phyllo cups until full then put banana sauce on top. Serve right away.

Nutrition:
Calories: 735
Carbohydrates: 82 g
Cholesterol: 111 mg
Fat: 45 g
Fiber: 3 g
Protein: 7 g
Sodium: 468 mg

148. Salmon Apple Salad Sandwich
Preparation Time: 15 minutes **Cooking Time:** 10 minutes **Servings:** 4

Ingredients:
- 4 ounces (125 g) canned pink salmon, drained and flaked
- 1 medium (180 g) red apple, cored and diced
- 1 celery stalk (about 60 g), chopped
- 1 shallot (about 40 g), finely chopped
- ⅓ cup (85 g) light mayonnaise
- 8 slices whole grain bread (about 30 g each), toasted
- 8 (15 g) Romaine lettuce leaves
- Salt and freshly ground black pepper

Directions:
1. Combine the salmon, apple, celery, shallot, and mayonnaise in a mixing bowl. Season with salt and pepper.
2. Place 1 slices bread on a plate, top with lettuce and salmon salad, and then covers with another slice of bread. Repeat procedure for the remaining ingredients.
3. Serve and enjoy.

Nutrition:
Calories: 315
Fat: 11.3 g
Carbohydrates: 40.4 g
Protein: 15.1 g
Sodium: 469 mg

149. Smoked Salmon and Cheese on Rye Bread
Preparation Time: 15 minutes **Cooking Time:** 10 minutes **Servings:** 4

Ingredients:
- 8 ounces (250 g) smoked salmon, thinly sliced
- ⅓ cup (85 g) mayonnaise
- 2 tablespoons (30 ml) lemon juice
- 1 tablespoon (15 g) Dijon mustard
- 1 teaspoon (3 g) garlic, minced
- 4 slices cheddar cheese (about 2 oz. or 30 g each)
- 8 slices rye bread (about 2 oz. or 30 g each)
- 8 (15 g) Romaine lettuce leaves
- Salt and freshly ground black pepper

Directions:
1. Mix the mayonnaise, lemon juice, mustard, and garlic in a small bowl. Flavor with salt and pepper and keep aside.
2. Spread dressing on 4 bread slices. Top with lettuce, salmon, and cheese. Cover with remaining rye bread slices.
3. Serve and enjoy.

Nutrition:
Calories: 365
Fat: 16.6 g
Carbohydrates: 31.6 g
Protein: 18.8 g
Sodium: 951 mg

150. Pan-Fried Trout
Preparation Time: 15 minutes **Cooking Time:** 10 minutes **Servings:** 4

Ingredients:
- 1 ¼ pounds trout fillets
- ⅓ cup white, or yellow, cornmeal
- ¼ teaspoon anise seeds
- ¼ teaspoon black pepper
- ½ cup minced cilantro, or parsley
- Vegetable cooking spray
- Lemon wedges

Directions:
1. Coat fish with combined cornmeal, spices, and cilantro, pressing it gently into fish. Set large skillet with cooking spray, heat over medium heat until hot.
2. Add fish and cook until fish is tender and flakes with fork, about 5 minutes on each side. Serve with lemon wedges.

Nutrition:
Calories: 207
Carbohydrates: 19 g
Cholesterol: 27 mg
Fat: 16 g
Fiber: 4 g
Protein: 18g

151. Lemon Cream Fruit Dip

Preparation Time: 5 minutes **Cooking Time:** 0 minutes **Servings:** 4

Ingredients:
- 1 cup (200 g) plain nonfat Greek yogurt
- ¼ cup (28 g) coconut flour 1 tbsp (15 ml) pure maple syrup
- ½ tsp. pure vanilla extract
- ½ tsp. pure almond extract
- Zest of 1 medium lemon
- Juice of ½ medium lemon

Directions:
1. In a medium bowl, merge together the yogurt, coconut flour, maple syrup, vanilla, almond extract, lemon zest, and lemon juice. Serve the dip with fruit or crackers.

Nutrition:
Calories: 80
Fat: 1g
Protein: 7g
Carbs: 10g
Sugar: 6g
Fiber: 3g
Sodium: 37mg

152. Greek Salad Kabobs

Preparation Time: 15 minutes **Cooking Time:** 0 minutes **Servings:** 24

Ingredients:

Dip:
- ¾ cup plain fat-free yogurt
- 2 teaspoons honey
- 2 teaspoons chopped fresh dill weed
- 2 teaspoons chopped fresh oregano leaves
- ¼ teaspoon salt
- 1 small clove garlic, finely chopped

Kabobs
- 24 cocktail picks or toothpicks
- 24 pitted kalamata olives
- 24 small grape tomatoes
- 12 slices (½ inch) English (seedless) cucumber, cut in half crosswise

Directions:
1. In small bowl, mix dip ingredients; set aside. 2 On each cocktail pick, thread 1 olive, 1 tomato and 1 half-slice cucumber. Serve kabobs with dip.

Nutrition:
Calories: 15
Fat: 0.5g
Protein: 0g
Carbohydrates: 2g
Sugars: 1g
Fiber: 0g
Sodium: 70mg

153. Green Goddess White Bean Dip

Preparation Time: 1 minute **Cooking Time:** 45 minutes **Servings:** 3

Ingredients:
- 1 cup dried navy, great Northern, or cannellini beans
- 4 cups water
- 2 teaspoons fine sea salt
- 3 tablespoons fresh lemon juice
- 1 tbsp. and ¼ cup extra-virgin olive oil
- ¼ cup firmly packed flat-leaf parsley leaves
- 1 bunch chives, chopped
- Leaves from 2 tarragon sprigs
- Freshly ground black pepper

Directions:
1. Combine the beans, water, and 1 teaspoon of the salt in the Instant Pot and stir to dissolve the salt.
2. Seal the lid and set the Pressure Release to Sealing. Press the Bean/Chili, Pressure Cook, or Manual setting and set the cooking time for 30 minutes at

high pressure if using navy or Great Northern beans or 40 minutes at high pressure if using cannellini beans.
3. When the cooking program is done, release the pressure naturally for 15 minutes. Unseal the pot and scoop out and reserve ½ cup of the cooking liquid.
4. In a food processor or blender, merge the beans, ½ cup cooking liquid, lemon juice, ¼ cup of olive oil, ½ tsp. parsley, chives, tarragon, remaining teaspoon salt, and ½ teaspoon pepper. Process or blend on medium speed, stopping to scrape down the sides of the container as needed, for about 1 minute, until the mixture is smooth.
5. Transfer the dip to a serving bowl. Set with the remaining 1 tbsp. olive oil and set with a few grinds of pepper. Serve at room temperature or chilled.

Nutrition:
Calories: 70
Fat: 5g
Protein: 3g
Carbohydrates: 8g
Sugars: 1g
Fiber: 4g
Sodium: 782mg

154. Vietnamese Meatball Lollipops with Dipping Sauce

Preparation Time: 30 minutes **Cooking Time:** 10 minutes **Servings:** 12

Ingredients:

Meatballs
- 1¼ lb. lean ground turkey
- ¼ cup chopped water chestnuts, drained
- ¼ cup hashed fresh cilantro
- 1 tbsp. cornstarch

Dipping Sauce
- ¼ cup water
- ¼ cup reduced-sodium soy sauce
- 2 tbsp. packed stevia
- 2 tbsp. chopped fresh chives or green onions

- 2 tbsp. fish sauce
- ½ tsp. pepper
- 3 cloves garlic, finely chopped

- 2 tbsp. lime juice
- 2 cloves garlic, finely chopped
- ½ tsp. crushed red pepper
- About 6-inch bamboo skewers

Directions:
1. Heat oven to 400F. Set cookie sheet with foil; spray with cooking spray (or use nonstick foil).
2. In large bowl, merge all meatball ingredients until well mixed. Form into 1¼-inch meatballs. On cookie sheet, set meatballs 1 inch apart. Bake 20 minutes, turning halfway through baking.
3. Meanwhile, in 1-quart saucepan, warmth all dipping sauce ingredients over low heat until stevia dissolved; keep aside.
4. Insert bamboo skewers into cooked meatballs; set on serving plate. Serve with dipping sauce.

Nutrition:
Calories: 80
Fat: 2.5g
Protein: 10g
Carbohydrates: 5g
Sugars: 1g
Fiber: 0g
Sodium: 440mg

155. Blackberry Baked Brie

Preparation Time: 5 minutes **Cooking Time:** 15 minutes **Servings:** 5

Ingredients:
- 8-ounce round Brie
- 1 cup water

- ¼ cup sugar-free blackberry preserves
- 2 teaspoons chopped fresh mint

Directions:
1. Strip a grid pattern into the top of the rind of the Brie with a knife.
2. In a 7-inch round baking dish, set the Brie, and then seal the baking dish securely with foil.
3. Set the trivet into the inner pot of the Instant Pot, spill in the water.
4. Make a foil sling and form it on top of the trivet. Set the baking dish on top of the trivet and foil sling.
5. Seal the lid to the locked position and turn the vent to sealing.
6. Choose the Manual and set the Instant Pot for 1 minutes on high pressure.
7. When cooking time is up, set off the Instant Pot and do a quick release of the pressure.
8. When the valve has dropped, detach the lid, and then remove the baking dish.
9. Detach the top rind of the Brie and top with the preserves. Set with the fresh mint.

Nutrition:
- Calories: 133
- Fat: 10g
- Protein: 8g
- Carbohydrates: 4g
- Sugars: 0g
- Fiber: 0g
- Sodium: 238mg

156. Creamy Spinach Dip

Preparation Time: 13 minutes **Cooking Time:** 5 minutes **Servings:** 11

Ingredients:
- 8 ounces low-fat cream cheese
- 1 cup low-fat sour cream
- ½ cup finely chopped onion
- ½ cup no-sodium vegetable broth
- 5 cloves garlic, minced
- ½ teaspoon salt
- ¼ teaspoon black pepper
- 10 ounces frozen spinach
- 12 ounces reduced-fat shredded Monterey Jack cheese
- 12 ounces reduced-fat shredded Parmesan cheese

Directions:
1. Attach cream cheese, sour cream, onion, vegetable broth, garlic, salt, pepper, and spinach to the inner pot of the Instant Pot.
2. Seal the lid, make sure vent is set to sealing, and set to the Bean/Chili setting on high pressure for 5 minutes.
3. When finished, do a manual release.
4. Attach the cheeses and mix well until creamy and well merged.

Nutrition:
- Calories: 274
- Fat: 18g
- Protein: 19g
- Carbohydrates: 10g
- Sugars: 3g
- Fiber: 1g
- Sodium: 948mg

157. Pesto Veggie Pizza

Preparation Time: 20 minutes **Cooking Time:** 15 minutes **Servings:** 2

Ingredients:
- Olive oil, for greasing the parchment paper
- ¼ head cauliflower, cut into florets
- 3 tablespoons almond flour
- ½ teaspoons olive oil
- 1 egg, beaten
- Minced garlic
- Pinch sea salt
- ¼ cup Simple Tomato Sauce (here)
- ¼ zucchini, thinly sliced
- ¼ cup baby spinach leaves
- 2 ½ asparagus spears, woody ends trimmed, cut into 3-inch pieces
- Basil pesto

Directions:
1. Preheat the oven to 450F. Put a baking sheet without a rim in the oven.
2. Prepare a piece of parchment paper by lightly brushing with olive oil and set aside.
3. Set a large saucepan filled halfway with water over high heat and bring it to a boil.
4. Set the cauliflower in a food processor, and pulse until very finely chopped, almost flour consistency.
5. Transfer the ground cauliflower to a fine-mesh sieve and put it over the boiling water for about 1 minute, until the cauliflower is cooked.
6. Wring out all the water from the cauliflower using a kitchen towel. Transfer the cauliflower to a large bowl.
7. Stir in the almond flour, oil, egg, garlic, and salt, and mix to create a thick dough. With your hands, press the ingredients together, and transfer the cauliflower mixture to the parchment paper.
8. Press the mixture out into a flat circle, about ½ inch thick. Slide the parchment paper onto the baking sheet in the oven.
9. Bake the crust.
10. Detach the crust from the oven and spread the sauce evenly to the edges of the crust.
11. Arrange the zucchini, spinach, and asparagus on the pizza.
12. Drizzle the pizza with basil pesto and put it back in the oven for about 2 minutes, until the vegetables are tender. Serve.

Nutrition:
Calories: 107 Fat: 7g
Protein: 5g Carbohydrates: 4g

158. Apple Leather

Preparation Time: 10 minutes **Cooking Time:** 8 to 10 hours **Servings:** 24 strips

Ingredients:
- 5 apples, peeled, cored, and sliced
- ¼ cup water
- 1 teaspoon pure vanilla extract
- ¼ teaspoon ground ginger
- ¼ teaspoon ground cloves

Directions:
1. Put the apples, water, vanilla, ginger, and cloves in a large saucepan over medium heat.
2. Set the mixture to a boil, reduce to low heat, and simmer for about 20 minutes, until the apples are very tender.
3. Set the apple mixture to a food processor, and purée until very smooth.
4. Set the oven on the lowest possible setting.
5. Line a baking sheet with parchment paper.
6. Pour the puréed apple mixture onto the baking sheet and spread it out very thinly and evenly.
7. Set the baking sheet, and bake for 8 to 10 hours, until the leather is smooth and no longer sticky.
8. Cut the apple leather with a pizza cutter into 2 strips, and store this treat in a container in a cool dark place for up to 2 weeks.

Nutrition:
Calories: 41 Fat: 0.3g
Protein: 0.1g Carbohydrates: 1.2g

159. French bread Pizza

Preparation Time: 5 minutes **Cooking Time:** 2-3 hours **Servings:** 2

Ingredients:
- ½ cup asparagus(diced)
- ½ cup Roma tomatoes(diced)
- ½ cup red bell pepper(diced)
- ½ tablespoon minced garlic
- ½ loaf French bread
- ½ cup pizza sauce
- ½ cup low-fat shredded mozzarella cheese

Directions:
1. Heat the oven to 400F. Coat the baking sheet lightly with a cooking spray.
2. Add the asparagus, tomatoes, and pepper in a little dish. Add the garlic and stir gently to coat uniformly.
3. Adjust the French bread to the baking sheet. Apply ¼ cup of the pizza sauce and ¼ of the vegetable paste to each portion of the mixture. Whisk with cup of mozzarella cheese.
4. Bake until the cheese is finely browned and the vegetables are tender for 8 to 10 minutes. Serve straight away.

Nutrition:
Calories: 265 Protein: 15g
Fat: 5g Carbohydrates: 2g

160. Candied Pecans

Preparation Time: 5 minutes **Cooking Time:** 11 minutes **Servings:** 6

Ingredients:
- 1 ½ tsp. butter
- 1 ½ cup pecan halves
- 2 ½ tbsp. Splenda, divided
- 1 tsp. cinnamon
- ¼ tsp. ginger
- ⅛ tsp. cardamom
- ⅛ tsp. salt

Directions:
1. In a small bowl, stir together 1 ½ teaspoons Splenda, cinnamon, ginger, cardamom and salt. Set aside.
2. Melt butter in a medium skillet over med-low heat. Add pecans, and two tablespoons Splenda. Reduce heat to low and cook, stirring occasionally, until sweetener dissolves, about 5 to 8 minutes.
3. Attach the spice mixture to the skillet and stir to coat pecans. Spread mixture to parchment paper and cool for 10-15 minutes. Store in an airtight container. Serving size is ¼ cup.

Nutrition:
Calories 173
Protein 2g
Fat 16g
Carbohydrates: 3.4g

Side Dishes

161. French Lentils

Preparation Time: 5 minutes **Cooking Time:** 25 minutes **Servings:** 10

Ingredients:
- 2 tablespoons olive oil
- 1 medium onion, diced
- 1 medium carrot, peeled and diced
- 2 cloves minced garlic
- 5 ½ cups water
- 2 ¼ cups French lentils, washed and drained
- 1 teaspoon dried thyme
- 2 small bay leaves
- Salt and pepper

Directions:
1. Warmth the oil in a saucepan over medium heat.
2. Attach the onions, carrot, and garlic and sauté for 3 minutes.
3. Stir in the water, lentils, thyme, and bay leaves – season with salt.
4. Set to a boil and cook until tender, about 20 minut
5. Drain any excess water and adjust seasoning to tas Serve hot.

Nutrition:
Calories: 185
Fat: 3.3g
Carbohydrates: 7.9
Protein: 11.4g
Sugar: 1.7g
Fiber: 13.7g
Sodium: 11mg

162. Grain-Free Berry Cobbler

Preparation Time: 5 minutes **Cooking Time:** 25 minutes **Servings:** 10

Ingredients:
- 4 cups fresh mixed berries
- ½ cup ground flaxseed
- ¼ cup almond meal
- ¼ cup unsweetened shredded coconut
- ½ tablespoon baking powder
- 1 teaspoon ground cinnamon
- ¼ teaspoon salt
- Powdered stevia, to taste
- 6 tablespoons coconut oil

Directions:
1. Warmth the oven to 375F and lightly grease a 10-inch cast-iron skillet.
2. Spread the berries on the bottom of the skillet.
3. Spill together the dry ingredients in a mixing bowl.
4. Cut in the coconut oil using a fork to create a crumbled mixture.
5. Set the crumble over the berries and bake for 25 minutes until hot and bubbling.
6. Cool the cobbler for 5 to 10 minutes before serving.

Nutrition:
Calories: 224 Fiber: 3.4g Sodium: 51mg
Fat: 17.5g Sugar: 3.3g
Carbohydrates: 10g Protein: 9.4g

163. Coffee-Steamed Carrots

Preparation Time: 10 minutes **Cooking Time:** 3 minutes **Servings:** 4

Ingredients:
- 1 cup brewed coffee
- 1 teaspoon Splenda brown sugar
- ½ teaspoon kosher salt
- Freshly ground black pepper
- 1-pound baby carrots
- Chopped fresh parsley
- 1 teaspoon grated lemon zest

Directions:
1. Pour the coffee into the electric pressure cooker. Stir in the brown sugar, salt, and pepper. Add the carrots.
2. Close the pressure cooker. Set to sealing.
3. Cook on high pressure for minutes.
4. Once complete, click Cancel and quick release the pressure.
5. Once the pin drops, open and remove the lid.
6. Using a slotted spoon, portion carrots to a serving bowl. Topped with the parsley and lemon zest and serve.

Nutrition:
Calories: 205 Fiber: 6.6g Sodium: 235mg
Fat: 12.5g Sugar: 5.3g
Carbohydrates: 15.1g Protein: 3.9g

164. Rosemary Potatoes

Preparation Time: 5 minutes **Cooking Time:** 25 minutes **Servings:** 2

Ingredients:
- 1lb red potatoes
- 1 cup vegetable stock
- 2tbsp olive oil
- 2tbsp rosemary sprigs

Directions:
1. Situate potatoes in the steamer basket and add the stock into the Instant Pot.
2. Steam the potatoes in your Instant Pot for 15 minutes.
3. Depressurize and pour away the remaining stock.
4. Set to sauté and add the oil, rosemary, and potatoes.
5. Cook until brown.

Nutrition:
Calories: 209 Sugar: 0.5g
Fat: 17g Carbohydrates: 5g
Protein: 6g

165. Kale and Cabbage Salad with Peanuts

Preparation Time: 15 minutes **Cooking Time:** 0 minutes **Servings:** 6

Ingredients:
- 2 bunches baby kale, thinly sliced
- ½ head green savoy cabbage, cored and thinly sliced

Dressing:
- ¼ cup apple cider vinegar
- Juice of 1 lemon
- 1 teaspoon ground cumin
- ¼ teaspoon smoked paprika
- 1 cup toasted peanuts
- 1 medium red bell pepper, thinly sliced
- 1 garlic clove, thinly sliced

Directions:
1. Toss the kale with cabbage in a large bowl. Set aside.
2. In a separate bowl, spill together the vinegar, lemon juice, cumin, and paprika until completely mixed.
3. Pour the dressing into the bowl of greens and using your hands to massage the greens until thickly coated.
4. Add the peanuts, bell peppers, and garlic to the bowl. Gently toss to combine well.
5. Serve chilled or at room temperature.

Nutrition:
Calories: 297
Fat: 4 g
Cholesterol: 276 mg
Sodium: 291 mg
Carbohydrates: 35 g
Sugar: 9 g
Protein: 29 g

166. Chili Lime Salmon

Preparation Time: 6 minutes **Cooking Time:** 10 minutes **Servings:** 2

Ingredients:

For Sauce:
- 1 jalapeno pepper
- 1 tablespoon chopped parsley
- 1 teaspoon minced garlic
- ½ teaspoon cumin
- ½ teaspoon paprika
- ½ teaspoon lime zest
- 1 tablespoon honey
- 1 tablespoon lime juice
- 1 tablespoon olive oil
- 1 tablespoon water

For Fish:
- 2 salmon fillets, each about 5 ounces
- 1 cup water
- ½ teaspoon salt
- ⅛ teaspoon ground black pepper

Directions:
1. Prepare salmon and for this, season salmon with salt and black pepper until evenly coated.
2. Plugin instant pot, insert the inner pot, pour in water, then place steamer basket and place seasoned salmon on it.
3. Seal instant pot with its lid, press the 'steam' button, then press the 'timer' to set the cooking time to 5 minutes and cook on high pressure, for 5 minutes.
4. Transfer all the ingredients for the sauce in a bowl, whisk until combined and set aside until required.
5. When the timer beeps, press 'cancel' button and do quick pressure release until pressure nob drops down.
6. Open the instant pot, then transfer salmon to serving plate and drizzle generously with prepared sauce.
7. Serve straight away.

Nutrition:
Calories: 224
Fat: 17.5g
Carbohydrates: 10g
Fiber: 3.4g
Sugar: 3.3g
Protein: 9.4g

167. Collard Greens

Preparation Time: 5 minutes **Cooking Time:** 6 hours **Servings:** 12

Ingredients:
- 2 pounds chopped collard greens
- ¾ cup chopped white onion
- 1 teaspoon onion powder
- 1 teaspoon garlic powder
- 1 teaspoon salt
- 2 teaspoons Splenda brown sugar

- ½ teaspoon ground black pepper
- ½ teaspoon red chili powder
- ¼ teaspoon crushed red pepper flakes
- 3 tablespoons apple cider vinegar
- 2 tablespoons olive oil
- 14.5-ounce vegetable broth
- ½ cup water

Directions:
1. Plugin instant pot, insert the inner pot, add onion and collard and then pour in vegetable broth and water.
2. Close instant pot with its lid, seal, press the 'slow cook' button, then press the 'timer' to set the cooking time to 6 hours at high heat setting.
3. When the timer beeps, press 'cancel' button and do natural pressure release until pressure nob drops down.
4. Open the instant pot, add remaining ingredients and stir until mixed.
5. Then press the 'sauté/simmer' button and cook for 3 to minutes or more until collards reach to desired texture.
6. Serve straight away.

Nutrition:
Calories: 228
Fat: 11.4g
Carbohydrates: 10.2g
Protein: 14.5g

168. Mashed Pumpkin

Preparation Time: 9 minutes   **Cooking Time:** 15 minutes   **Servings:** 2

Ingredients:
- 2 cups chopped pumpkin
- 0.5 cup water
- 2tbsp powdered sugar-free sweetener of choice
- 1tbsp cinnamon

Directions:
1. Place the pumpkin and water in your Instant Pot.
2. Seal and cook on Stew 15 minutes.
3. Remove and mash with the sweetener and cinnamon.

Nutrition:
Calories: 40
Fat: 2.5g
Carbohydrates: 3.3g
Protein: 2.5g

169. Turkey Loaf

Preparation Time: 10 minutes   **Cooking Time:** 50 minutes   **Servings:** 2

Ingredients:
- ½ lb. 93% lean ground turkey
- ⅓ cup panko breadcrumbs
- ½ cup green onion
- 1 egg
- ½ cup green bell pepper
- 1 tbsp. ketchup
- ¼ cup sauce (Picante)
- ½ tsp. cumin (ground)

Directions:
1. Preheat oven to 350F. Mix lean ground turkey, 3 tbsp Picante sauce, panko breadcrumbs, egg, chopped green onion, chopped green bell pepper and cumin in a bowl (mix well).
2. Put the mixture into a baking sheet; shape into an oval (about 1,5 inches thick). Bake 45 minutes.
3. Mix remaining Picante sauce and the ketchup; apply over loaf. Bake 5 minutes longer. Let stand 5 minutes.

Nutrition:
Calories 136
Protein 2g
Fat 6g
Carbohydrates: 3.2g

170. Mushroom Pasta

Preparation Time: 7 minutes   **Cooking Time:** 10 minutes   **Servings:** 4

Ingredients:
- 4 oz. whole-grain linguine
- 1 tsp. extra virgin olive oil
- ½ cup light sauce
- 2 tbsp. green onion
- 1 (8-oz) pkg. mushrooms
- 1 clove garlic
- ⅛ tsp. salt
- ⅛ tsp. pepper

Directions:
1. Cook pasta according to package Directions, drain.
2. Fry sliced mushrooms 4 minutes.

3. Stir in fettuccine minced garlic, salt and pepper. Cook 2 minutes.
4. Heat light sauce until heated; top pasta mixture properly with sauce and with finely-chopped green onion.

Nutrition:
Calories: 125
Protein: 20g
Fat: 4g
Carbohydrates: 1.2g

171. Garlic Kale Chips

Preparation Time: 6-7 minutes **Cooking Time:** 5 minutes **Servings:** 2

Ingredients:
- 1 tbsp. yeast flakes
- Sea salt to taste
- 4 cups packed kale
- 2 tbsp. olive oil
- 1 tsp. garlic, minced
- ½ cup ranch seasoning pieces

Directions:
1. In a bowl, set the oil, kale, garlic, and ranch seasoning pieces. Attach the yeast and mix well. Set the coated kale into an air fryer basket and cook at 375F for minutes.
2. Shake after 3 minutes and serve.

Nutrition:
Calories: 50
Total Fat: 1.9 g
Carbohydrates: 10 g
Protein: 46 g

172. Garlic Salmon Balls

Preparation Time: 6-7 minutes **Cooking Time:** 10 minutes **Servings:** 2

Ingredients:
- 6 oz. tinned salmon
- 1 large egg
- 3 tbsp. olive oil
- 5 tbsp. wheat germ
- ½ tsp. garlic powder
- 1 tbsp. dill, fresh, chopped
- 4 tbsp. spring onion, diced
- 4 tbsp. celery, diced

Directions:
1. Preheat your air fryer to 370F. In a large bowl, merge the salmon, egg, celery, onion, dill, and garlic.
2. Form the mixture into golf ball size balls and twirl them in the wheat germ. In a pan, warm olive oil over medium-low heat. Attach the salmon balls and slow flatten them. Set them to your air fryer and cook for 10 minutes.

Nutrition:
Calories: 219 Total Fat: 7.7 g
Carbohydrates: 14.8 g Protein: 23.1 g

173. Onion Rings

Preparation Time: 7 minutes **Cooking Time:** 10 minutes **Servings:** 3

Ingredients:
- 1 onion, cut into slices, then form into rings
- 1 ½ cup almond flour
- ¾ cup pork rinds
- 1 cup milk
- 1 egg
- 1 tbsp. baking powder
- ½ tsp. salt

Directions:
1. Warmth your air fryer for 10 minutes. In a container, merge the flour, baking powder, and salt.
2. Spill the eggs and the milk, then combines with flour. Gently soak the floured onion rings into the batter to coat them.
3. Set the pork rinds on a plate and dredge the rings the crumbs. Cook the onion rings in your air fryer for 10 minutes at 360F.

Nutrition:
Calories: 304
Total Fat: 18g
Carbohydrates: 31g
Protein: 38g

174. Crispy Eggplant Fries

Preparation Time: 7 minutes **Cooking Time:** 12 minutes **Servings:** 3

Ingredients:
- 2 eggplants
- ¼ cup olive oil
- ¼ cup almond flour
- ½ cup water

Directions:
1. Preheat your air fryer to 390F. Cut the eggplants into ½-inch slices. In a mixing bowl, merge the flour, olive oil, water, and eggplants.
2. Slowly coat the eggplants. Attach eggplants to the air fryer and cook for 12 minutes. Serve with yogurt or tomato sauce.

Nutrition:
Calories: 103
Fat: 7.3 g
Carbohydrates: 12.3 g
Protein: 1.9 g

175. Charred Bell Peppers

Preparation Time: 7 minutes **Cooking Time:** 4 minutes **Servings:** 3

Ingredients:
- 20 bell peppers, sliced and seeded
- 1 tsp. olive oil
- 1 pinch sea salt
- 1 lemon
- Pepper

Directions:
1. Preheat your air fryer to 390F. Set the peppers with oil and salt. Cook the peppers in the air fryer.
2. Set peppers in a bowl, and squeeze lemon juice over the top. Season with salt and pepper.

Nutrition:
Calories: 30
Fat: 0.25 g
Carbohydrates: 6.91 g
Protein: 1.28 g

176. Garlic Tomatoes

Preparation Time: 7 minutes **Cooking Time:** 15 minutes **Servings:** 4

Ingredients:
- 3 tbsp. vinegar
- ½ tsp. thyme, dried
- 4 tomatoes
- 1 tbsp. olive oil
- Salt and black pepper to taste
- 1 garlic clove, minced

Directions:
1. Preheat your air fryer to 390F. Scratch the tomatoes into halves and detach the seeds. Set them in a big bowl and toss them with oil, salt, pepper, garlic, and thyme.
2. Set them into the air fryer and cook for 15 minutes. Drizzle with vinegar and serve.

Nutrition:
Calories: 28.9
Fat: 2.4 g
Carbohydrates: 2.0 g
Protein: 0.4 g

177. Mushroom Stew

Preparation Time: 7 minutes **Cooking Time:** 1 hour 22 minutes **Servings:** 3

Ingredients:
- 1 lb. chicken, cubed, boneless, skinless
- 2 tbsp. canola oil
- 1 lb. fresh mushrooms, sliced
- 1 tbsp. thyme, dried
- ¼ cup water
- 2 tbsp. tomato paste
- 4 garlic cloves, minced
- 1 cup green peppers, sliced
- 3 cups zucchini, diced
- 1 large onion, diced
- 1 tbsp. basil
- 1 tbsp. marjoram
- 1 tbsp. oregano

Directions:
1. Divide the chicken into cubes. Set them in the air fryer basket and pour olive oil over them. Attach

mushrooms, zucchini, onion, and green pepper. Merge and add garlic, cook for 2 minutes, then add tomato paste, water, and seasonings.

2. Seal the air fryer and cook the stew for 50 minutes Set the heat to 340F and cook.
3. Detach from air fryer and transfer into a large pan Empty in a bit of water and simmer for 10 minutes.

Nutrition:
Calories: 53
Fat: 3.3 g
Carbohydrates: 4.9 g
Protein: 2.3 g

178. Cheese and Onion Nuggets

Preparation Time: 7 minutes **Cooking Time:** 12 minutes **Servings:** 4

Ingredients:
- 7 oz. Edam cheese, grated
- 2 spring onions, diced
- 1 egg, beaten
- 1 tbsp. coconut oil
- 1 tbsp. thyme, dried
- Salt and pepper to taste

Directions:
1. Merge the onion, cheese, coconut oil, salt, pepper, thyme in a bowl. Set 8 small balls and place the cheese in the center.
2. Set in the fridge for about an hour. With a pastry brush, carefully garnish the beaten egg over the nuggets. Cook in the air fryer at 350F.

Nutrition:
Calories: 227
Fat: 17.3 g
Carbohydrates: 4.5 g
Protein: 14.2 g

179. Spiced Nuts

Preparation Time: 7 minutes **Cooking Time:** 25 minutes **Servings:** 3

Ingredients:
- 1 cup almonds
- 1 cup pecan halves
- 1 cup cashews
- 1 egg white, beaten
- ½ tsp. cinnamon, ground
- Pinch cayenne pepper
- ¼ tsp. cloves, ground
- Pinch salt

Directions:
1. Combine the egg white with spices. Preheat your air fryer to 300F.
2. Spill the nuts in the spiced mixture. Cook for 25 minutes, stir throughout cooking time.

Nutrition:
Calories: 88.4
Fat: 7.6 g
Carbohydrates: 3.9 g
Protein: 2.5 g

180. Keto French fries

Preparation Time: 7 minutes **Cooking Time:** 20 minutes **Servings:** 4

Ingredients:
- 1 large rutabaga, peeled, divided into spears about ¼-inch wide
- Salt and pepper to taste
- ½ tsp. paprika
- 2 tbsp. coconut oil

Directions:
1. Preheat your air fryer to 450F. Mix the oil, paprika, salt, and pepper.
2. Spill the oil mixture over the rutabaga fries. Cook for 20 minutes.

Nutrition:
Calories: 113
Fat: 7.2g
Carbohydrates: 12.5g
Protein: 1.9g

Appetizer

181. Calico Slaw

Preparation Time: 5 minutes **Cooking Time:** 5 minutes **Servings:** 8

Ingredients:

- 1 Red Delicious apple, cored and chopped
- 1 Golden Delicious apple, cored and chopped
- ½ teaspoon of fine sea salt
- 1 medium head green cabbage, shredded
- 3 carrots, shredded
- 2 tablespoons of apple cider vinegar
- 2 tablespoons of stevia
- 1 green bell pepper
- 1 red bell pepper
- 1 yellow bell pepper
- ground black pepper, to taste

Directions:

1. Combine carrots, cabbage, green bell pepper, red bell pepper, Red Delicious apple, and Golden Delicious apple in a bowl.
2. Whisk apple cider vinegar, sea salt, and stevia in a bowl; season with black pepper.
3. Pour vinegar mixture over cabbage mixture.
4. Stir gently to coat.
5. Seal the bowl and set to refrigerator for at least 30 minutes.
6. Serve and enjoy!

Nutrition:
Calories: 315
Fat: 11.3 g
Carbohydrates: 40.4 g
Protein: 15.1 g
Sodium: 469 mg

182. Simple Appetizer Meatballs

Preparation Time: 25 minutes **Cooking Time:** 25 minutes **Servings:** 24 pieces

Ingredients:
- ½ pound lean ground beef
- ½ pound lean ground pork
- ½ cup sodium-free chicken broth
- ¼ cup almond flour
- 1 tablespoon low-sodium tamari sauce
- ½ teaspoon ground cumin
- ¼ teaspoon freshly ground black pepper

Directions:
1. Preheat the oven to 375F.
2. Combine all the Ingredients together until completely incorporated in a large bowl.
3. Roll the mixture into ¾-inch balls and place them on a parchment-lined baking sheet.
4. Bake the meatballs until they are ready through and golden brown.
5. Serve.

Nutrition:
Calories: 125
Protein: 20g
Fat: 4g
Carbohydrates: 1.2g

183. Chicken Souvlaki Salad

Preparation Time: 20 minutes **Cooking Time:** 10 minutes **Servings:** 2

Ingredients:
- 2 cups of romaine lettuce, bite-sized
- ½ cup of cocktail or cherry tomatoes
- ¼ English cucumber, thickly sliced
- 1 teaspoon of dried oregano (divided)
- ¼ teaspoon of kosher salt
- 2 tablespoons of crumbled feta cheese
- ¾ pound of skinless and boneless chicken breast (divided into 1-inch cubes)
- zest from ½ lemon
- 1 tablespoon of freshly squeezed lemon juice (divided)
- 2 tablespoons of extra-virgin olive oil (divided)
- freshly ground pepper
- ¼ cup of Easy Instant Pot Yogurt (or store-bought yogurt)

Directions:
1. In a bowl, combine the lemon zest, chicken, ½ tablespoon lemon juice, ½ teaspoon oregano, ½ tablespoon olive oil, salt and a few grinds of pepper.
2. Let the chicken marinate for about 10 minutes.
3. Preheat a skillet over medium-high heat. Add ½ tbsp. of olive oil, then add the chicken.
4. Stir for about 8 minutes, then transfer to a plate lined with paper towels.
5. In another bowl, combine ½ tablespoon lemon juice, the yogurt, tablespoon olive oil, ½ teaspoon oregano and a few grinds of pepper.
6. In a bowl, mix the lettuce with a few tablespoons of dressing.
7. Divide the lettuce between two bowls and add the chicken, cucumbers, tomatoes, and feta cheese.
8. Serve and enjoy!

Nutrition:
Calories: 113
Fat: 7.2 g
Carbohydrates: 12.5
Protein: 1.9 g

184. Celery with Chickpea Feta Salad

Preparation Time: 15 minutes **Cooking Time:** 0 minutes **Servings:** 3

Ingredients:
For the salad:
- 5 ounces of small tomatoes (grape, cherry, etc.) halved or quartered
- ½ cup of feta cheese crumbled

For the dressing:
- 1 teaspoon garlic pepper
- 1 tablespoon balsamic vinegar
- 4 (3-inches) sprigs thyme
- 1 (15-ounces) can of chickpeas rinsed and drained
- 2 stalks celery sliced
- 2 tablespoons extra-virgin olive oil

Directions:
Making the dressing:

1. In a glass jar, mix the oil, vinegar, and pepper.

Making the salad:
1. In a bowl, combine the celery, chickpeas, and tomatoes.
2. Add the feta and seasoning.

2. Shake until well combined.
3. Add the leaves to the salad and discard the stems.
4. Distribute the chickpea salad in serving bowls. Serve and enjoy!

Nutrition:
Calories: 71
Fat: 4.8g
Carbohydrates: 6.6g
Fiber: 2.3g

185. Basil Vinaigrette with Summer Corn Salad

Preparation Time: 15 minutes **Cooking Time:** 0 minutes **Servings:** 6

Ingredients:
- 2 to 3 large spring onions thinly sliced (white part only)
- 1 cup of cucumber chopped
- 2 radishes thinly sliced into half-moons
- kosher salt
- ½ cup of avocado oil or extra-virgin olive oil
- 4 large ears of corn husks and silks were removed, cooked
- 1 large tomato seeded and chopped
- freshly ground black pepper
- 2 tablespoons of white wine vinegar
- ¼ cup of chopped fresh basil

Directions:
1. In a bowl, whisk together the vinegar, avocado oil, and basil
2. Add the corn to the bowl with the oil mixture.
3. Add the onion, tomatoes, cucumber, and radishes to the bowl.
4. Merge well and season with salt and pepper.
5. Serve immediately and enjoy. Or refrigerate for up to 24 hours.

Nutrition:
Calories: 40
Fat: 2.5g
Carbohydrates: 3.3g
Fiber: 0.9g

186. Lemon Vinaigrette with Sugar Snap Pea Salad

Preparation Time: 20 minutes **Cooking Time:** 2 minutes **Servings:** 3

Ingredients:
- 2 cups of alfalfa sprouts
- 2 tablespoons of fresh chives chopped
- 2 teaspoon of sugar snap peas
- 2 small radishes diced
- 2 tablespoons of Lemon Vinaigrette

Directions:
1. Set a pot of water to a boil.
2. Fill a bowl with ice water and place a small strainer in the bowl.
3. Attach the peas to the boiling water and cook for 2 minutes.
4. Drain the peas and lay them out on a clean dish towel, and dry.
5. Place the peas in a bowl and add the radishes.
6. Stir in 2 tablespoons of the dressing.
7. Divide sprouts among 4 salad plates: top with pea mixture.
8. Sprinkle with chives. Serve and enjoy!

Nutrition:
Calories: 53
Fat: 3.3 g
Carbohydrates: 4.9 g
Protein: 2.3 g

187. Green Dressing with Shrimp Avocado Salad

Preparation Time: 5 minutes **Cooking Time:** 5 minutes **Servings:** 4

Ingredients:
Green dressing:
- 3 tablespoons of extra-virgin olive oil divided
- ½ teaspoon of salt
- Freshly ground black pepper
- 2 oranges
- ½ cup of parsley
- 2 scallions roughly chopped
- ¼ cup of canned unsweetened coconut cream

Salad:
- ¼ cup of unsalted cashews toasted and roughly chopped
- 4 radishes thinly sliced
- 1 ½ pounds of large shrimp 31-40 count, peeled and deveined
- 12 cups of salad greens, you can use baby red and green romaine
- 1 avocado chopped

Directions:
Making the dressing:
1. Use a small knife to skin the orange starting at the top and cut along the orange's length.
2. Do this all the way around, making sure to remove the white pith. Repeat with other oranges.
3. Cut between the membranes of the orange to remove the segments again.
4. Squeeze the juice from the remaining orange membranes into a blender container.
5. If there is juice on your cutting board, add that to the blender as well. Discard the membranes.
6. Add the scallions, parsley, coconut cream, tablespoon olive oil, salt, and a few pinches of pepper to the blender container.
7. Puree until smooth. Set aside.

Making the salad:
1. From a double layer of paper towels on a plate. Set aside.
2. Season shrimp with a few grinds of pepper. Warmth a wok over medium-high heat and add 1 tablespoon olive oil.
3. Attach half the shrimp and stir-fry until opaque, about 2 minutes.
4. Detach to plate and repeat with remaining shrimp and 1 tablespoon olive oil.
5. Attach salad greens to a large bowl and toss with some of the dressing. Set greens on 4 serving plates and add orange segments, avocado, cashew, radishes, and shrimp.
6. Set with remaining dressing and enjoy!

Nutrition:
Calories: 193
Fat: 5.5 g
Protein: 10 g
Carbohydrates: 1.9g

188. Beans with Pearl Couscous

Preparation Time: 10 minutes **Cooking Time:** 5 minutes **Servings:** 4

Ingredients:
For the dressing:
- ⅛ teaspoon of kosher salt
- 2 tablespoons of extra-virgin olive oil
- 3 tablespoons of cider vinegar
- 1 teaspoon of dried basil leaves
- 1 garlic clove finely minced

For the salad:
- 1 cup of grape or cherry tomatoes quartered
- ½ cup of chopped onion
- 14 ounces of beans (cannellini, Great Northern, black, kidney, or a mixture), rinsed and drained 1 can
- 1 ¼ cups of water
- 4 ounces of uncooked whole-wheat pearl couscous
- 1 hothouse cucumber diced
- 2 ounces of mozzarella cheese "pearls" or fresh mozzarella cheese diced

Directions:
1. In a bowl, whisk together basil, vinegar, garlic, and salt.
2. Continue whisking and attach the oil in a steady stream. Set aside.
3. Set water to a boil in a saucepan.
4. Attach the couscous, cover, and cook over low heat until tender.
5. Leak run under cold water and let drain again while you prepare the salad.
6. In a bowl, mix tomatoes, cucumbers, onion, beans and cheese. Add cooled couscous and dressing.
7. Stir and serve immediately.

Nutrition:
Calories: 209
Fat: 17g
Protein: 6g
Sugar: 0.5g
Carbohydrates: 5g

189. Blackened Chicken Breast with Jalapeno Caesar Salad

Preparation Time: 8 minutes **Cooking Time:** 5 minutes **Servings:** 4

Ingredients:

- 1 small jalapeño pepper with some of the seeds, quartered
- 3 large cloves of garlic
- ¼ cup of grated Parmigiano-Reggiano cheese
- 1 large 18-ounces bunch of romaine lettuce, roughly chopped and chilled
- 2 tablespoons of Dijon mustard
- 1 pound of boneless skinless chicken breasts
- 1 ½ teaspoons of extra-virgin olive oil
- 1 teaspoon of freshly ground black pepper divided
- 1 ½ tablespoons of Worcestershire sauce
- 4 ounces of organic silken tofu drained (½ cup)

Directions:

1. Preheat the grill. Pound the chicken until about ½ inch thick.
2. Rub chicken with ½ teaspoon oil and sprinkle with ¾ teaspoon pepper.
3. Bake the chicken breasts on a baking sheet, about 8 minutes.
4. Let cooked chicken rest for at least 5 minutes, then slice into thin strips.
5. Add the garlic, jalapeño, cheese, mustard, Worcestershire sauce, tofu, and remaining ¼ teaspoon black pepper to a blender and blend.
6. Add 1 teaspoon oil and blend until smooth.
7. Mix the dressing with the chicken strips and lettuce and serve. Enjoy

Nutrition:
Calories 253
Protein 15g
Fat 20g
Carbohydrates: 2.1g

190. Ginger Dressing with Kale Chicken Salad

Preparation Time: 5 minutes **Cooking Time:** 12 minutes **Servings:** 4

Ingredients:

- ¾ cup of light raspberry salad dressing
- 2 to 3 teaspoons of grated ginger root
- 1 pound of boneless skinless chicken breast
- 8 cups of packed spinach with baby kale greens

Directions:

1. Heat a skillet with medium-high heat.
2. Set chicken with cooking spray and sprinkle with a pinch of salt and pepper, if desired. Cook and allow to cool and thinly slice.
3. Arrange equal amounts of vegetables and chicken on four plates. Whisk together salad dressing and ginger until well blended.
4. Spoon equal amounts into the mixture. Serve.

Nutrition:
Calories: 228
Total Fats: 11.4g
Carbohydrates: 10.2g
Protein: 14.5g

191. Asian Cucumber Salad

Preparation Time: 5 minutes **Cooking Time:** 5 minutes **Servings:** 4

Ingredients:

For the dressing:

- ¼ cup of rice vinegar
- Dash of crushed red pepper
- 1 tbsp. of low-sodium tamari or soy sauce
- 2 teaspoons of sesame oil
- 2 teaspoons of honey

For the salad:

- 2 medium scallions (thinly sliced)
- 2 teaspoons black sesame seeds
- 1 pound English cucumbers (spiralized or sliced)
- 2 carrots (spiralized or grated)

Directions:

1. Spill together the tamari or soy sauce, sesame oil, honey, rice vinegar, and crushed red pepper in a large bowl.
2. Attach the sliced or spiralized cucumbers, spiralized or grated carrots, and sliced scallions.
3. Merge until the vegetables are well-coated
4. Garnish with sesame seeds.
5. Serve and enjoy!

Nutrition:
Calories: 50
Total Fat: 1.9 g
Carbohydrates: 10 g
Protein: 46 g

192. Pecans with Blackberry Ginger Beet Salad

Preparation Time: 60 minutes **Cooking Time:** 10 minutes **Servings:** 6

Ingredients:
- 1 tablespoon of whole-grain mustard
- 6 cups of mixed salad greens
- Coarse kosher salt
- Freshly ground black pepper
- 4 ounces of fresh goat cheese
- 1 pound of fresh beets washed and trimmed
- ⅓ cup + 2 tbsp. extra virgin olive oil plus for drizzling on beets before roasting
- 1 cup of whole pecans
- ¼ cup + 2 tablespoons blackberry ginger balsamic vinegar or any other fruity balsamic

Directions:
1. Preheat oven to 425F. Place beets on aluminum foil, drizzle with a little olive oil, and wrap tightly. Form the package on a baking sheet and roast for 1 hour or until the beets are tender. Allow cooling.
2. Next, heat a skillet over medium-high heat. Add pecans and stir until toasted. Remove from heat and allow to cool.
3. In another bowl, spill together the mustard and ¼ cup balsamic vinegar. Slowly spill in ⅓ cup olive oil, constantly whisking, until mixture has thickened.
4. In another bowl, whisk together 2 tablespoons olive oil and 2 tablespoons balsamic vinegar.
5. Skin the beets and cut them into thick slices.
6. Add to the vinegar/olive oil mixture.
7. Set the salad with some of the dressing and season with salt and pepper.
8. Arrange the greens on 4 individual serving plates. Add the beets, goat cheese, and toasted pecans. Serve.

Nutrition:
Calories: 224
Fat: 17.5g
Carbohydrates: 10g
Fiber: 3.4g

193. Blueberry Watermelon Salad

Preparation Time: 15 minutes **Cooking Time:** 0 minutes **Servings:** 4

Ingredients:
- zest from ½ lemon
- fresh mint chopped (optional)
- 1 pound of watermelon cut into small chunks (about half of a small melon)
- 1 cup of blueberries
- Kosher salt

Directions:
1. Set watermelon and blueberries in a large bowl.
2. Lightly drizzle with salt.
3. Merge gently enough that you won't nick the blueberries.
4. Brush with lemon zest and mint, if desired.

Nutrition:
Calories: 735
Carbohydrates: 82 g
Fat: 45 g
Fiber: 3 g

194. Orange Vinaigrette with Roasted Beets

Preparation Time: 20 minutes **Cooking Time:** 60 minutes **Servings:** 8

Ingredients:
- ¼ cup of squeezed orange juice
- 1 small shallot (minced)
- 1 clove garlic (minced)
- 2 tablespoons of rice vinegar
- ½ teaspoon of ground cumin
- ¼ teaspoon of ground coriander
- 1 pound of golden beets (washed and trimmed)
- 1 pound of red beets (washed and trimmed)
- ¼ cup of olive oil plus ⅓ cup (divided)
- ¼ teaspoon of kosher salt
- Freshly ground black pepper
- 1 teaspoon of Dijon mustard
- 1 tablespoon of parsley (chopped)

Directions:

1. Preheat oven to 350F.
2. Place the beets in a bowl. Attach the salt, pepper, and olive oil, then mix well.
3. Wrap each beet in aluminum foil, then place it on a baking sheet.
4. Bring in the oven and roast for about 1 hour or until the beets are soft.
5. Detach from oven and set aside to cool.
6. Place the shallots, orange juice, garlic, rice vinegar, cumin, and cilantro in a small saucepan over medium heat.
7. Set everything to a boil, then reduce the heat to medium-low and let the mixture simmer until its volume has reduced by half, about 10 minutes.
8. Remove from heat and allow cooling.
9. After about 5 minutes, attach the mustard to the mixture, olive oil while whisking constantly.
10. Remove the skins from each beet and discard.
11. Cut the beets into chunks, and then place them in a bowl and mix with the desired amount of dressing.
12. Garnish with parsley. Serve and enjoy!

Nutrition:
Calories: 71
Fat: 4.8g
Carbohydrates: 6.6g
Fiber: 2.3g

195. Blueberries with Nectarines Spinach Salad

Preparation Time: 15 minutes **Cooking Time:** 5 minutes **Servings:** 6

Ingredients:
- Freshly ground black pepper
- ¾ pound of fresh blueberries
- ¾ pound of fresh nectarines pitted and cut into ½-inch chunks
- 10 cups of baby spinach
- 2 tablespoons of balsamic vinegar, you can use blackberry ginger
- 3 tablespoons of extra virgin olive oil
- 1 shallot cut in half lengthwise and then thinly sliced
- 1 teaspoon of coarse kosher salt
- 1 cup of slivered almonds

Directions:
1. In a bowl, spill together oil, vinegar, shallots, salt, and pepper.
2. Add blueberries and nectarines and their juice.
3. Spill to coat and let sit for at least 10 minutes. Add the almonds, spinach and stir until the leaves are covered in the dressing.
4. Serve and enjoy!

Nutrition:
Calories: 258.1
Fat: 13 g
Protein: 18.2 g
Carbohydrates: 7g

196. Taco Slaw

Preparation Time: 20 minutes **Cooking Time:** 0 minutes **Servings:** 6

Ingredients:
- 1 carrot, chopped
- 1 tablespoon of chopped fresh cilantro
- 1 lime, juiced
- ½ small head cabbage, chopped
- 1 jalapeno pepper, seeded and minced
- ½ red onion, minced

Directions:
1. Mix the cabbage, carrot, cilantro, lime juice, jalapeno pepper, and red onion in a bowl. Serve!

Nutrition:
Calories: 45
Fat: 1 g
Protein: 2 g
Carbohydrates: 6.1g

197. Egg Fried Veg

Preparation Time: 10 minutes **Cooking Time:** 7 minutes **Servings:** 2

Ingredients:
- 4oz egg whites
- 1 cup mixed vegetables
- 2tbsp milk
- zero calorie spray
- herb and spice mix

Directions:
1. Spray a heat-proof bowl that fits in your Instant Pot with nonstick spray.
2. Whisk together the eggs, milk, and seasoning.
3. Pour into the bowl. Add the vegetables.

4. Place the bowl in your steamer basket.
5. Spill 1 cup of water into your Instant Pot.
6. Lower the basket into your Instant Pot.
7. Seal and cook on low pressure for 7 minutes.
8. Depressurize quickly.
9. Stir well and allow to rest, it will finish cooking in its own heat.

Nutrition:
Calories: 281
Protein: 4g
Fat: 23g
Carbohydrates: 5g

198. Bone Broth

Preparation Time: 10 minutes **Cooking Time:** 60 minutes **Servings:** 2

Ingredients:
- 1 chicken carcass and dripping OR 1 large marrow bone
- 1 chopped onion
- 1 stalk chopped celery
- 1tbsp minced garlic
- 1tbsp bouillon powder

Directions:
1. Place the chicken, onion, and celery in your Instant Pot.
2. Cover with 2 cups of water.
3. Seal and cook for 60 minutes.
4. Release the pressure naturally.
5. Strain the solids out.
6. Add the garlic and bouillon.

Nutrition:
Calories: 258.1
Fat: 13 g
Protein: 18.2 g
Carbohydrates: 7g

199. Cauliflower and Celeriac Soup

Preparation Time: 15 minutes **Cooking Time:** 10 minutes **Servings:** 2

Ingredients:
- 0.5lb cauliflower, chopped
- 4oz celeriac, chopped
- 1 chopped onion
- 2 cups vegetable stock
- salt and pepper

Directions:
1. Mix all the ingredients in your Instant Pot.
2. Cook on Stew for 10 minutes.
3. Depressurize naturally and blend.

Nutrition:
Calories: 40
Fat: 2.5g
Carbohydrates: 3.3g
Fiber: 0.9g

200. Mushroom and Eggs

Preparation Time: 10 minutes **Cooking Time:** 7 minutes **Servings:** 2

Ingredients:
- 4oz egg whites
- 1 cup chopped brown mushrooms
- 2tbsp milk
- zero calorie spray
- 1tsp mustard

Directions:
1. Spray a heat-proof bowl that fits in your Instant Pot with nonstick spray.
2. Whisk together the eggs, milk, and seasoning.
3. Pour into the bowl. Add the mushroom.
4. Place the bowl in your steamer basket.
5. Spill 1 cup of water into your Instant Pot.
6. Lower the basket into your Instant Pot.
7. Seal and cook on low pressure for 7 minutes. Depressurize quickly.
8. Stir well and allow to rest, it will finish cooking in own heat.

Nutrition:
Calories: 85
Protein: 3g
Fat: 3g
Carbohydrates: 6g

Dessert

201. Strawberry Chiffon Pie

Preparation Time: 15 minutes **Cooking Time:** 45 minutes **Servings:** 4

Ingredients:

- 1 cup of crushed pineapple, unsweetened
- 12 strawberries
- 1 packet of O-Zenta strawberry gelatin
- 7 packages of artificial sweetener
- 1 cup of evaporated skim milk, chilled
- 1 tablespoon of lemon juice
- 1 ½ teaspoon of vanilla
- 1 teaspoon of almond extract

Directions:

1. Bring pineapple to a boil. Stir in gelatin, strawberries, and sweetener.
2. Stir until gelatin is completely dissolved.
3. Whisk milk and lemon juice in a cooled bowl until frothy.
4. Add the extracts and beat until stiff.
5. Slowly attach the gelatin mixture to the whipp[ed] milk.
6. Add to a 10-inch pie plate and refrigerate for a f[ew] minutes
7. Garnish with additional strawberries.
8. Serve and enjoy!

Nutrition:
Calories: 212
Carbohydrates: 4.8g
Protein: 14.3g
Sugar: 1.1g

202. Strawberry Fruit Squares

Preparation Time: 40 minutes **Cooking Time:** 45 minutes **Servings:** 4-6

Ingredients:

- 2 envelopes dietetic strawberry gelatin
- 1 cup of boiling water
- 1 cup of crushed pineapple in own juice
- 1 ripe banana, finely diced
- 6 ounces of plain yogurt
- 1 envelope Sweet and Low

Directions:

1. Set gelatin in boiling water.
2. Attach juice drained from pineapple with cold water.
3. Set cold water to equal 1 cup liquid.
4. Attach pineapple and banana. Pour ½ into a 1-quart bowl.
5. Chill until firm. Spread with plain yogurt mixed with a sugar substitute.
6. Place bowl in the freezer for 30 minutes until yogurt is firmer.
7. Pour remaining gelatin, very carefully, on top.
8. Chill until firm. Cut in squares.
9. Serve and enjoy!

Nutrition:

Calories: 250
Fat: 9 g
Protein: 3 g
Carbohydrates: 4.1g

203. Copper Penny Carrots

Preparation Time: 40 minutes **Cooking Time:** 45 minutes **Servings:** 15

Ingredients:

- 2 pounds carrots, cleaned and sliced thin
- 1 green pepper, thinly sliced

Sauce:

- ¼ cup of salad oil
- 1 teaspoon of Worcestershire sauce
- 1 (10 ounces of) can tomato soup, undiluted
- 1 medium onion, thinly sliced
- Salt and pepper as desired
- 1 teaspoon of yellow mustard
- ½ cup of vinegar
- 20 packets Equal

Directions:

1. Start cooking carrots in a covered pot in ½ inch of water, 11 minutes after boiling begins so carrots will be tender but not crispy.
2. Rinse in cold water to stop cooking. In a bowl, alternate layers of vegetables.
3. For the Sauce, mix all the ingredients.
4. Bring sauce ingredients to a boil. Remove from heat.
5. Cool for a few minutes. Add 20 equal packets. Place in blender and blend.
6. Pour sauce over vegetables while still hot. Cool.
7. Refrigerate at least 12 hours before serving.
8. Keep in refrigerator for several weeks in a covered plastic container.
9. To serve, use a slotted spoon. Serve!

Nutrition:

Calories: 48
Carbohydrates: 11g
Protein: 3g

204. Poached Pears

Preparation Time: 20 minutes **Cooking Time:** 1 hour 15 minutes **Servings:** 6

Ingredients:

- 6 medium ripe pears (about 2 pounds)
- 5 cups of white, unsweetened grape juice
- ¼ cup of fresh lemon juice
- 1 vanilla bean, split lengthwise
- 1-inch whole cinnamon stick
- ¼ cup of golden raisins

Directions:

1. The first thing to do is to skin the pears but leave the stems.
2. Mix the juices, vanilla bean, and cinnamon stick in a medium-sized pan and then cook over low heat.
3. Add the pears. Simmer uncovered for about 30 minutes, turning pears occasionally until tender when pierced with a knife.
4. Remove pears.
5. Reduce syrup for about 30 to 35 min to 1 ½ cups. Strain.
6. Stir in raisins and cool syrup to room temperature.
7. Serve pears in small glass compound bowls.
8. Spoon raisins and syrup over and around pears.

Nutrition:
Calories: 79
Fat: 2g
Carbohydrates: 8g
Protein: 10g

205. Carrot Cake

Preparation Time: 10 minutes **Cooking Time:** 40 minutes **Servings:** 18

Ingredients:
- Margarine and flour for pan
- 1 ½ cup of all-purpose flour
- ¼ cup of whole wheat flour
- 1 teaspoon of baking powder
- ½ teaspoon of baking soda
- ½ teaspoon of ground cinnamon
- ½ teaspoon of ground ginger
- 2 tablespoons of stevia; 2 eggs; vegetable oil.
- ¼ cup of unsweetened pineapple juice concentrate
- 1 teaspoon of vanilla extract
- 1 cup of shredded carrots
- ½ cup of golden raisins; salt
- ½ cup of unsweetened, crushed pineapple, drained

Directions:
1. Warmth oven to 350 F. Grease and flour a 9 X 5 X 3 inches loaf pan.
2. In bowl, merge flours, baking powder, baking soda, cinnamon, ginger, and salt.
3. In a second bowl, spill oil, stevia, eggs, pineapple juice, and vanilla.
4. Stir liquid into dry ingredients until smooth. Stir carrots, raisins, and pineapple.
5. Scrape into prepared pan. Bake for 35 to 40 minutes.
6. Set cake and ice with Cream Cheese Frosting. Cut into ½ inches slices to serve.

Nutrition:
Calories: 71
Fat: 4.8g
Carbohydrates: 6.6g
Fiber: 2.3g

206. Bran Muffins

Preparation Time: 10 minutes **Cooking Time:** 40 minutes **Servings:** 12

Ingredients:
- 1 cup of bran
- cup of buttermilk
- banana, mashed well
- 1 egg
- ¼ cup of oil
- ¼ cup of honey
- 1 cup of whole wheat flour
- 1 teaspoon of baking soda
- Pinch of salt
- 2 tablespoons of margarine
- 2 tablespoons of honey

Directions:
1. Mix first 9 ingredients together. Place in microwave muffin pan.
2. Microwave 3 ½ mins. Mix last 2 ingredients together.
3. Spoon on each muffin and return to micro-wave for 1 minute.
4. Serve and enjoy!

Nutrition:
Calories 65
Protein 2g
Fat 1g
Carbohydrates: 2.4g

207. Frozen Mocha Milkshake

Preparation Time: 5 minutes **Cooking Time:** 0 minutes **Servings:** 1

Ingredients:
- 1 cup (240 ml) unsweetened vanilla almond milk
- 3 tbsp. (18 g) unsweetened cocoa powder
- 2 tsp. (4 g) instant espresso powder
- 1½ cups (210 g) crushed ice
- ½ medium avocado, peeled and pitted
- 1 tbsp. (15 ml) pure maple syrup
- 1 tsp. pure vanilla extract

Directions:
1. In a blender, combine the almond milk, cocoa powder, espresso powder, ice, avocado, maple syrup, and vanilla. Blend the ingredients on high speed 60 seconds, until the milkshake is smooth.

Nutrition:

Calorie: 307
Fat: 20g
Protein: 6g
Carbohydrates: 33g
Sugars: 13g
Fiber: 13g
Sodium: 173mg

208. Baked Berry Cups with Crispy Cinnamon Wedges

Preparation Time: 25 minutes **Cooking Time:** 30 minutes **Servings:** 4

Ingredients:

- 2 tsp. stevia
- ¾ tsp. ground cinnamon
- Butter-flavor cooking spray
- 1 balanced carb whole wheat tortilla
- ¼ cup stevia
- 2 tbsp. white whole wheat flour
- 1 tsp. grated orange peel, if desired
- 1½ cups fresh blueberries
- 1½ cups fresh raspberries
- About 1 cup fat-free whipped cream topping

Directions:

1. Heat oven to 375F. In sandwich-size resealable food-storage plastic bag, merge 2 teaspoons stevia and ½ tsp. of the cinnamon. Set both sides of tortilla, about 3 seconds per side; divide tortilla into 8 wedges. In bag with cinnamon-sugar, attach wedges, seal bag. Shake to coat wedges evenly.
2. On ungreased cookie sheet, spread out wedges. Bake 7 to 9 minutes.
3. Meanwhile, spray custard cups or ramekins with cooking spray; place cups on another cookie sheet. In small bowl, spill ¼ cup stevia, the flour, orange peel and remaining ¼ teaspoon cinnamon until blended. In medium bowl, gently whisk berries with stevia mixture; divide evenly among custard cups.
4. Bake 15 minutes; stir gently.
5. To serve, set each cup with about ¼ cup whipped cream topping; serve tortilla wedges with berry cups. Serve warm.

Nutrition:

Calories: 735
Carbohydrates: 82 g
Fat: 45 g
Fiber: 3 g

209. Berry Smoothie Pops

Preparation Time: 5 minutes **Cooking Time:** 0 minutes **Servings:** 6

Ingredients:

- 2 cups frozen mixed berries
- ½ cup unsweetened plain almond milk
- 1 cup plain nonfat Greek yogurt
- 2 tablespoons hemp seeds

Directions:

1. Set all the ingredients in a blender and process until finely blended.
2. Pour into 6 clean ice pop molds and insert sticks.
3. Freeze for 3 to 4 hours.

Nutrition:

Calories: 70
Fat: 2g
Protein: 5g
Carbohydrates: 9g
Sugars: 2g
Fiber: 3g
Sodium: 28mg

210. Instant Pot Tapioca

Preparation Time: 10 minutes **Cooking Time:** 7 minutes **Servings:** 6

Ingredients:

- 2 cups water
- 1 cup small pearl tapioca
- ½ cup stevia
- 4 eggs
- ½ cup evaporated skim milk
- ¼ cup substitute sugar (like stevia)
- 1 teaspoon vanilla
- Fruit of choice, optional

Directions:

1. Combine water and tapioca in Instant Pot.
2. Secure lid. Press Manual and set for 5 minutes.
3. Perform a quick release. Press Cancel, remove lid, and press Sauté.
4. Whisk together eggs and evaporated milk. SLOWLY attach to the Instant Pot, stirring constantly so the eggs don't scramble.
5. Stir in the sugar substitute until it's dissolved, press Cancel, then stir in the vanilla.

6. Allow to cool thoroughly, then refrigerate at least 4 hours.

Nutrition:
Calories: 267
Fat: 18g
Carbohydrates: 26g
Protein: 2g

211. Oatmeal Cookies

Preparation Time: 5 minutes **Cooking Time:** 15 minutes **Servings:** 6

Ingredients:
- ¾ cup almond flour
- ¾ cup old-fashioned oats
- ¼ cup shredded unsweetened coconut
- 1 teaspoon baking powder
- 1 teaspoon ground cinnamon
- ¼ teaspoon salt
- ¼ cup unsweetened applesauce
- 1 large egg
- 1 tablespoon pure maple syrup
- 2 tablespoons coconut oil, melted

Directions:
1. Preheat the oven to 350F.
2. In a medium mixing bowl, merge the almond flour, oats, coconut, baking powder, cinnamon, and salt, and mix well.
3. In another medium bowl, combine the applesauce, egg, maple syrup, and coconut oil, and mix. Stir the wet mixture into the dry mixture.
4. Form the dough into balls. Bake for 12 minutes.
5. Using a spatula, remove the cookies and cool on rack.

Nutrition:
Calories: 76
Fat: 6g
Protein: 2g
Carbohydrates: 5g
Sugars: 1g
Fiber: 1g
Sodium: 57mg

212. Raspberry Nice Cream

Preparation Time: 5 minutes **Cooking Time:** 0 minutes **Servings:** 3

Ingredients:
- 2 cups frozen, sliced, overripe bananas
- 2 cups frozen or fresh raspberries
- Pinch of sea salt
- 1-2 tablespoons coconut nectar or 1-1½ tablespoons pure maple syrup

Directions:
1. In a food processor or high-speed blender, combine the bananas, raspberries, salt, and 1 tablespoon of the nectar or syrup. Puree until smooth. Taste, and add the remaining nectar or syrup, if desired.
2. Serve immediately, if you like a soft-serve consistency, or transfer to an airtight container and freeze for an hour or more, if you like a firm texture.

Nutrition:
Calorie: 193
Fat: 1g
Protein: 3g
Carbohydrates: 47g
Sugars: 24g
Fiber: 13g
Sodium: 101mg

213. Chocolate Baked Bananas

Preparation Time: 10 minutes **Cooking Time:** 10-15 minutes **Servings:** 8

Ingredients:
- 4-5 large ripe bananas, sliced lengthwise
- 2 tbsp. coconut nectar or pure maple syrup
- 1 tablespoon cocoa powder
- Couple pinches sea salt
- 2 tablespoons nondairy chocolate chips (for finishing)
- 1 tablespoon chopped pecans, walnuts, almonds, pumpkin seeds (for finishing)

Directions:
1. Set a baking sheet with parchment paper and preheat oven to 450F.
2. Bring bananas on the parchment. In a bowl, merge the coconut nectar or maple syrup with the cocoa powder and salt. Whisk well to fully combine. Set chocolate mixture over the bananas.
3. Bake for 8 to 10 minutes. Set on chocolate chips and nuts and serve.

Nutrition:

Calories: 146　　Carbohydrates: 34g　　Sodium: 119mg
Fat: 3g　　Sugars: 18g
Protein: 2g　　Fiber: 4g

214. Greek Yogurt Berry Smoothie Pops

Preparation Time: 5 minutes　　**Cooking Time:** 0 minutes　　**Servings:** 6

Ingredients:

- 2 cups frozen mixed berries
- ½ cup unsweetened plain almond milk
- 1 cup plain nonfat Greek yogurt
- 2 tablespoons hemp seeds

Directions:

1. Set all the ingredients in a blender and process until finely blended.
2. Pour into 6 clean ice pop molds and insert sticks.
3. Freeze for 3 to 4 hours.

Nutrition:

Calories: 70　　Carbohydrates: 9g　　Sodium: 28mg
Fat: 2g　　Sugar: 2g
Protein: 5g　　Fiber: 3g

215. Grilled Peach and Coconut Yogurt Bowls

Preparation Time: 5 minutes　　**Cooking Time:** 10 minutes　　**Servings:** 4

Ingredients:

- 2 peaches, halved and pitted
- ½ cup plain nonfat Greek yogurt
- 1 teaspoon pure vanilla extract
- ¼ cup unsweetened dried coconut flakes
- 2 tablespoons unsalted pistachios, shelled and broken into pieces

Directions:

1. Preheat the broiler to high. Arrange the rack in the closest position to the broiler.
2. In a shallow pan, arrange the peach halves, cut-side up. Broil for 6 to 8 minutes until browned, tender, and hot.
3. In a small bowl, mix the yogurt and vanilla.
4. Spoon the yogurt into the cavity of each peach half.
5. Sprinkle 1 tablespoon of coconut flakes and 1½ teaspoons of pistachios over each peach half. Serve warm.

Nutrition:

Calories: 102　　Carbohydrates: 11g　　Sodium: 12mg
Fat: 5g　　Sugars: 8g
Protein: 5g　　Fiber: 2g

216. Frozen Chocolate Peanut Butter Bites

Preparation Time: 5 minutes　　**Cooking Time:** 0 minutes　　**Servings:** 32

Ingredients:

- 1 cup coconut oil, melted
- ¼ cup cocoa powder
- ¼ cup honey
- ¼ cup natural peanut butter

Directions:

1. Spill the melted coconut oil into a bowl. Whisk in the cocoa powder, honey, and peanut butter.
2. Transfer the mixture to ice cube trays in portions about 1½ teaspoons each.
3. Freeze for 2 hours or until ready to serve.

Nutrition:

Calories: 80　　Carbohydrates: 3g　　Sodium: 20mg
Fat: 8g　　Sugars: 2g
Protein: 1g　　Fiber: 0g

217. Dark Chocolate Almond Butter Cups

Preparation Time: 15 minutes　　**Cooking Time:** 0 minutes　　**Servings:** 12

Ingredients:

- ½ cup natural almond butter
- 1 tablespoon pure maple syrup
- 1 cup dark chocolate chips
- 1 tablespoon coconut oil

Directions:

1. Set a 12-cup muffin tin with cupcake liners.

2. In a medium bowl, mix the almond butter and maple syrup. If necessary, heat in the microwave to soften slightly.
3. Spoon about 2 teaspoons of the almond butter mixture into each muffin cup and press down to fill.
4. In a double boiler or the microwave, dissolve the chocolate chips. Stir in the coconut oil and mix well to incorporate.
5. Drop 1 tablespoon of chocolate on top of each almond butter cup.
6. Freeze for at least 30 minutes to set. Thaw for 10 minutes before serving.

Nutrition:
Calories: 101
Fat: 8g
Protein: 3g
Carbohydrates: 6g
Sugars: 4g
Fiber: 1g
Sodium: 32mg

218. No-Bake Carrot Cake Bites

Preparation Time: 15 minutes **Cooking Time:** 0 minutes **Servings:** 20

Ingredients:
- ½ cup old-fashioned oats
- 2 medium carrots, chopped
- 6 dates, pitted
- ½ cup chopped walnuts
- ½ cup coconut flour
- 2 tablespoons hemp seeds
- 2 teaspoons pure maple syrup
- 1 teaspoon ground cinnamon
- ½ teaspoon ground nutmeg

Directions:
1. In a blender jar, combine the oats and carrots, and process until finely ground. Transfer to a bowl.
2. Add the dates and walnuts to the blender and process until coarsely chopped. Return the oat-carrot mixture to the blender and add the coconut flour, hemp seeds, maple syrup, cinnamon, and nutmeg. Process until well mixed.
3. Set the dough into balls about the size of tablespoon.
4. Store in the refrigerator in an airtight container for up to 1 week.

Nutrition:
Calories: 68
Fat: 3g
Protein: 2g
Carbohydrates: 10g
Sugars: 6g
Fiber: 2g
Sodium: 6mg

219. Creamy Strawberry Crepes

Preparation Time: 10 minutes **Cooking Time:** 10 minutes **Servings:** 4

Ingredients:
- ½ cup old-fashioned oats
- 1 cup unsweetened plain almond milk
- 1 egg
- 3 teaspoons honey, divided
- Nonstick cooking spray
- 2 ounces (57 g) low-fat cream cheese
- ¼ cup low-fat cottage cheese
- 2 cups sliced strawberries

Directions:
1. In a blender jar, process the oats until they resemble flour. Add the almond milk, egg, and 1½ teaspoons honey, and process until smooth.
2. Heat a large skillet over medium heat. Spray with nonstick cooking spray to coat.
3. Add ¼ cup of oat batter to the pan and quickly swirl around and cook for 2 to 3 minutes.
4. Clean the blender jar, and then combine the cream cheese, cottage cheese, and remaining 1½ teaspoons honey, and process until smooth.
5. Set each crepe with 2 tablespoons of the cream cheese mixture, topped with ¼ cup of strawberries. Serve.

Nutrition:
Calories: 149
Fat: 6g
Protein: 6g
Carbohydrates: 20g
Sugars: 10g
Fiber: 3g
Sodium: 177mg

220. Swirled Cream Cheese Brownies

Preparation Time: 10 minutes **Cooking Time:** 20 minutes **Servings:** 12

Ingredients:

- 2 eggs
- ¼ cup unsweetened applesauce
- ¼ cup coconut oil, melted
- 3 tablespoons pure maple syrup, divided
- ¼ cup unsweetened cocoa powder
- ¼ cup coconut flour
- ¼ teaspoon salt
- 1 teaspoon baking powder
- 2 tablespoons low-fat cream cheese

Directions:

1. Preheat the oven to 350F (180C). Grease an 8-by-8-inch baking dish.
2. In a mixing bowl, set the eggs with the applesauce, coconut oil, and 2 tablespoons of maple syrup.
3. Stir in the cocoa powder and coconut flour and mix well. Sprinkle the salt and baking powder evenly over the surface and mix well to incorporate. Set the mixture to the prepared baking dish.
4. In a small, microwave-safe bowl, microwave the cream cheese for 10 to 20 seconds until softened. Add the remaining 1 tablespoon of maple syrup and mix to combine.
5. Drop the cream cheese onto the batter and use a toothpick or chopstick to swirl it on the surface. Bake for 20 minutes.
6. Store refrigerated in a seal container for up to 5 days.

Nutrition:

Calories: 84 Carbohydrates: 6g Sodium: 93mg
Fat: 6g Sugars: 4g
Protein: 2g Fiber: 2g

Index

Air Fryer Brussels sprouts; 69
Air Fryer Lemon Cod; 57
Amazing Overnight Apple and Cinnamon Oatmeal; 33
Apple and Pumpkin Waffles; 13
Apple Cinnamon Chia Pudding; 10
Apple Cinnamon Oatmeal; 31
Apple Leather; 77
Asian Cucumber Salad; 90
Autumn Pork Chop with Red Cabbage and Apples; 34
Autumn Pork Chops; 45
Baked Berry Cups with Crispy Cinnamon Wedges; 97
Baked Eggplant with Marinara; 65
Baked Potato Topped with Cream cheese 'n Olives; 63
Baked Zucchini Recipe from Mexico; 62
Banana and Zucchini Bread; 17
Banana Crêpe Cakes; 14
Banana Nut Bread; 23
Banana Pepper Stuffed with Tofu 'n Spices; 63
Barbecue Turkey Burger Sliders; 47
Basic Bread Stuffing; 24
Basil Vinaigrette with Summer Corn Salad; 88
Basil-Parmesan Crusted Salmon; 57
Beans with Pearl Couscous; 89
Beef and Pepper Fajita Bowls; 41
Beef and Red Bean Chili; 38
Beef Massaman Curry; 37
Beef steaks with green asparagus; 30
Bell Pepper-Corn Wrapped in Tortilla; 64
Bell Peppered Rings with Egg and Avocado Salsa; 10
Berry Smoothie Pops; 97
Black Bean Burger with Garlic-Chipotle; 64
Blackberry Baked Brie; 75
Blackened Chicken Breast with Jalapeno Caesar Salad; 90
Blueberries with Nectarines Spinach Salad; 92
Blueberry and Chicken Salad; 21
Blueberry Watermelon Salad; 91
Bone Broth; 93
Bran Muffins; 96
Breakfast Cheddar Zucchini Casserole; 16
Breakfast Grain Porridge; 17
Broccoli Beef Stir-Fry; 40
Broccoli Omelet; 30
Bruschetta Chicken; 49
Brussels sprouts with Balsamic Oil; 63
Buckwheat Crêpes; 13
Cajun Catfish; 59
Cajun Flounder and Tomatoes; 60
Cajun Shrimp; 57

Cajun Shrimp and Roasted Vegetables; 60
Calico Slaw; 86
Candied Pecans; 77
Carrot Cake; 96
Cauliflower and Celeriac Soup; 93
Celery with Chickpea Feta Salad; 87
Charred Bell Peppers; 84
Cheese and Onion Nuggets; 85
Cheeseburger Pie; 71
Cheesy Cauliflower Fritters; 68
Chicken and Broccoli Bake; 50
Chicken and Mushrooms; 70
Chicken and Veggies Bake; 50
Chicken Souvlaki Salad; 87
Chicken with Bell Peppers; 51
Chicken with Bok Choy; 52
Chicken with Broccoli and Mushroom; 53
Chicken with Cabbage; 52
Chicken with Caper Sauce; 49
Chicken with Mushrooms; 52
Chicken with Olives; 51
Chicken with Yellow Squash; 53
Chicken with Zucchini Noodles; 53
Chili Lime Salmon; 81
Chipotle Chili Pork Chops; 42
Chocolate Baked Bananas; 98
Cider Pork Stew; 39
Cilantro and Lime Broccoli Rice; 27
Cilantro Lime Grilled Shrimp; 60
Citrus and Chicken Salad; 21
Clear soup with liver dumplings; 29
Coconut Meringue Cake; 23
Coconut Shrimp; 55
Coffee-Steamed Carrots; 80
Collard Greens; 81
Colorful vegetable casserole; 28
Copper Penny Carrots; 95
Cottage Pancakes; 12
Crab Frittata; 61
Creamy Spinach and Mushroom Lasagna; 66
Creamy Spinach Dip; 76
Creamy Strawberry Crepes; 100
Crispy Air Fryer Fish; 57
Crispy Eggplant Fries; 84
Crispy Fish Sticks; 56
Crispy Jalapeno Coins; 68
Crispy-Topped Baked Vegetables; 65
Crunchy Lemon Shrimp; 61

Cuban Pulled Pork Sandwich; 39
Dark Chocolate Almond Butter Cups; 99
Dill Pickle Dip; 24
Egg Fried Veg; 92
Egg Salad Sandwiches; 16
Fish and Chips; 58
Fish Nuggets; 59
French bread Pizza; 77
French Lentils; 79
Fresh Pot Pork Butt; 44
Frozen Chocolate Peanut Butter Bites; 99
Frozen Mocha Milkshake; 96
Funnel Cakes; 25
Garlic Kale Chips; 83
Garlic Rosemary Grilled Prawns; 59
Garlic Salmon Balls; 83
Garlic Tomatoes; 84
Ginger Dressing with Kale Chicken Salad; 90
Glazed Bananas in Phyllo Nut Cups; 72
Grain-Free Berry Cobbler; 80
Greek Baklava; 72
Greek Salad Kabobs; 74
Greek Yogurt and Oat Pancakes; 12
Greek Yogurt Berry Smoothie Pops; 99
Green Dressing with Shrimp Avocado Salad; 88
Green Goddess White Bean Dip; 74
Green Salad with Berries and Sweet Potatoes; 19
Grilled Peach and Coconut Yogurt Bowls; 99
Grilled Salmon with Lemon; 58
Grilled Tuna Steaks; 61
Halibut with Lime and Cilantro; 34
Honey Garlic Butter Roasted Carrots; 28
Honey-Glazed Salmon; 56
Hummus; 67
Instant Pot Tapioca; 97
Jicama Fries; 69
Joseph's Bacon; 22
Kale and Cabbage Salad with Peanuts; 81
Keto French fries; 85
Lemon Cream Fruit Dip; 74
Lemon Vinaigrette with Sugar Snap Pea Salad; 88
Lentil snack with tomato salsa; 29
Lime-Parsley Lamb Cutlets; 42
Loaded Cottage Pie; 43
Mashed Pumpkin; 82
Meat skewers with polenta; 41
Meatballs Barley Soup; 37
Melon Cucumber Salad; 72
Mouth-Watering Egg Casserole; 32
Mushroom and Eggs; 93
Mushroom Frittata; 14
Mushroom Pasta; 82
Mushroom Stew; 84
No-Bake Carrot Cake Bites; 100
Nutty Steel-cut Oatmeal with Blueberries; 31

Oatmeal Cookies; 98
Old Fashioned Beef Soup with Vegetables; 38
Onion Rings; 83
Orange Vinaigrette with Roasted Beets; 91
Orange-Marinated Pork Tenderloin; 34
Oyster Stew; 23
Pan-Fried Trout; 73
Pecan-Oatmeal Pancakes; 24
Pecans with Blackberry Ginger Beet Salad; 91
Pesto Chicken Bake; 50
Pesto Veggie Pizza; 76
Poached Pears; 95
Pork Chops Pomodoro; 36
Pork Diane; 44
Pork Medallions with Cherry Sauce; 36
Portobello and Chicken Sausage Frittata; 15
Rainbow Bean Salad; 20
Raspberry Choco Oatmeal; 11
Raspberry Nice Cream; 98
Roasted Chickpea; 22
Roasted Root Vegetables; 67
Roasted Squash Puree; 67
Rosemary Potatoes; 80
Salad with Salsa Verde Vinaigrette; 12
Salmon Apple Salad Sandwich; 73
Salmon Cakes; 55
Salmon Cream Cheese and Onion on Bagel; 71
Salmon Feta and Pesto Wrap; 71
Salmon Fillets; 58
Seasoned Chicken Breast; 48
Shrimp Burgers; 25
Shrimp Peri-Peri; 33
Shrimp with Scallion Grits; 16
Shrimps Saganaki; 26
Simple Appetizer Meatballs; 87
Simple Beef Roast; 28
Slow "Roasted" Tomatoes; 31
Smoked Salmon and Cheese on Rye Bread; 73
Smothered Sirloin; 43
Spaghetti Squash Tots; 69
Spiced Chicken Breast; 48
Spiced Nuts; 85
Spicy Garlic Pasta; 28
Strawberry Chiffon Pie; 94
Strawberry Fruit Squares; 95
Sugar Free Strawberry Cheesecake; 26
Sunday Pot Roast; 40
Swirled Cream Cheese Brownies; 101
Taco Slaw; 92
Tacos with Pico De Gallo; 15
Texas Goulash; 22
Thai Roasted Veggies; 68
Three Bean and Scallion Salad; 20
Tomato Waffles; 17
Tomato-Herb Omelet; 32

Traditional Beef Stroganoff; 42
Tropical Yogurt Kiwi Bowl; 14
Turkey and Quinoa Caprese Casserole; 47
Turkey Chili; 46
Turkey Divan Casserole; 48
Turkey Loaf; 82
Vegan Edamame Quinoa Collard Wraps; 64
Veggie Fillets Omelets; 11
Vietnamese Meatball Lollipops with Dipping Sauce; 75
Warm Barley and Squash Salad; 20
Whole Wheat Chapatti; 25
Yogurt and Parmesan Chicken Bake; 49
Zoodles with Pea Pesto; 33
Zucchini Parmesan Chips; 66

Conclusion

Type 2 diabetes is a severe disease - not something to treat lightly. As you learned from our 3 weeks to optimal blood sugar diet, a healthy lifestyle is a must if you want to control your diabetes. You need to realize that you can't just eat healthy foods to lose weight and control your blood sugar. You need to do the work if you want the results.

Now that you have read through our Type 2 Diabetes Cookbook, you know the basics of how to lose weight and control your blood pressure, cholesterol, and blood sugar. You can now take advantage of all these great benefits for yourself. You also need to realize that your age and weight will determine the time your body needs to adjust. Therefore, we propose sticking with the diet for three weeks. Not only will you feel greater, but your insulin levels will also begin to stabilize, and this will lower your chances of developing complications. Remember that the older you get, the more serious the condition. Therefore, those over 40 and overweight people should keep a close eye on their blood sugar and their medications.

This cookbook recipe section will show you how to transition your healthy lifestyle habits from a cookbook recipe method to a lifestyle guide. This guide is going to be very simple. It's going to be a day-by-day guide to help you begin your journey towards a healthier life. Let's start by talking about what you will need to be successful for this program to work. You will need something easy for you to stick with and something that you can stick with the rest of your life. The method of this is straightforward, and you will want to follow our lifestyle guide. Following the lifestyle guide will make your life healthier, happier, and more fulfilling. This book is planned to help you feel better, look better, and socialize better. It's simple. We are not trying to brainwash you with some weird cult ideals or anything like that. Our idea is that if it feels good for you, it must be suitable for your body. This book is designed to help you lose weight, lower your cholesterol, and lower your blood pressure. If you are seeking for a miracle cure to rid you of all these conditions at once, then this book may not be suitable for you. We don't expect everyone to follow our methods in the way we have laid them out for you. We hope that if you can open your mind to the possibilities, it will be easier for you to set up the diet plan that works well for your lifestyle. We want to help you take what we have learned and create your diet plan. You will need to take the information we have given you and mold it to fit your personal needs and wants.

It doesn't matter what category of diet plan you currently use. We all know that what we put into our body can either make it sick or make it feel good. We want to take what we learned from this book and help you form your recipe for healthy living.

This book has requested time and effort to be assembled and published.
If you have enjoyed it and it made some impact in your life, I would really be thankful if you can drop a review on the Amazon store, scanning with your phone camera the QR code below:

Thank you

Printed in Great Britain
by Amazon